Contents

Author's foreword **2**

North American Edition

Copyright © 2016 text AG&G Books

The right of David Squire to be identified as author of this work has been asserted by him in accordance with the Copyright, Designs and Patents Act 1988.

Copyright © 2016 illustrations and photographs IMM Lifestyle Books

Copyright © 2016 IMM Lifestyle Books

Designed and created for IMM Lifestyle Books by AG&G Books. Copyright © 2004, 2016 "Specialist" AG&G Books

Design: Glyn Bridgewater; Illustrations: Dawn Brend, Gill Bridgewater and Coral Mula; Editor: Alison Copland; Photographs: see page 80

Current Printing (last digit)
10 9 8 7 6 5 4 3 2 1

Printed in Singapore

Home Gardener's Container Gardens: Planting in containers and designing, improving and maintaining container gardens is published by Creative Homeowner under license with IMM Lifestyle Books.

ISBN: 978-1-58011-759-3

Creative Homeowner®, www.creativehomeowner.com, is distributed exclusively in North America by Fox Chapel Publishing Company, Inc., 800-457-9112, 1970 Broad Street, East Petersburg, PA 17520.

Author's foreword

Growing plants in containers has never been more popular and has enabled many people – often without a garden and perhaps with only a balcony, courtyard or small patio – to garden and derive enjoyment from growing plants. It has also made gardening possible for wheelchair gardeners and other people who are not as active as they were in earlier years.

The range of containers for plants is wide and encompasses window boxes and hanging baskets, perhaps the most popular and visually exciting ways to grow plants in containers. Wall baskets, troughs, tubs, urns and Versailles planters are other popular containers, as well as growing-bags for vegetables, herbs, spring bulbs and summer-flowering bedding plants.

There is almost no end to the range of containers and plants; strawberries in planters and barrels, apple trees in tubs and large terracotta pots, pouches hanging from walls and fences and packed with summer-flowering trailing and cascading plants, wheelbarrows burgeoning with summer flowers and stone sinks decked in miniature conifers, alpines and diminutive bulbs; they are all part of the passion for gardening in containers.

This inspirational all-color book guides novice gardeners through the "getting started" stage of container gardening, as well as providing exciting yet practical ideas for developing their hobby. If you love plants and aspire to creating a container garden, this is an exciting book to have at your elbow.

About the author

David Squire has a lifetime's experience with plants, both cultivated and native types. Throughout his gardening and journalistic careers, David has written more than 80 books on plants and gardening, including 14 books in this Specialist Guide series. He also has a wide interest in the uses of native plants, whether for eating and survival, or for their historical roles in medicine, folklore and customs.

SEASONS

Throughout this book, advice is given about seasonal tasks. Because of global and even regional variations in climate and temperature, the four main seasons have been used, with each subdivided into "early," "mid-" and "late" – for example, early spring, mid-spring and late spring. These 12 divisions of the year can be applied to the appropriate calendar months in your local area, if you find this helps.

Measurements

Both metric and US measurements are given in this book – for example, 6 ft (1.8 m).

Growing plants in containers

A popular way to grow plants is to plant them in a wide range of attractive containers and place these on patios and terraces, as well as in courtyards and many other places in a garden. Containers range from hanging baskets and window boxes, which bring color at waist or head height, to others for placing on the ground or even decorating balconies, edges of garage roofs, porches and verandas. Some can be used to decorate the sides of steps.

What is container gardening?

CONTAINERS IN GARDENS

- The range of containers used in gardens is wide and many are illustrated and described on pages 4–5. Some are used for single-season plants, such as summer-flowering bedding plants, while others create homes for all-season plants like small shrubs, trees and conifers.
- Do not confuse "growing plants in containers" in your garden with buying "container-grown" plants from garden centers. Container-grown plants are removed from their containers and planted into garden soil. Alternatively, they can be planted into decorative containers.

WHY GROW PLANTS IN CONTAINERS?

There are both advantages and disadvantages to growing plants in containers and here are a few of them.

Advantages:
- Plants can be positioned where you want them – often near to a house so that they can be easily seen.
- Fragrant plants are readily appreciated.
- Changes can be made from one season to another.
- Success does not depend on the quality of garden soil – it may be infested by pests and diseases.

Disadvantages:
- Plants need regular watering, especially in summer and where the amount of potting soil is small.
- Regular care and attention is essential for many plants.
- Range of plants is limited to those that flourish in small amounts of potting soil.

Water features

Miniature ponds in stone sinks and wooden tubs are possible on a patio (see page 66).

Pebble ponds where fountains spray water over pebbles in a shallow base – these are ideal features where toddlers live because, at worst, they only get wet.

Hanging baskets help to create interest above ground level.

Balcony gardening

Container gardening is ideal for balconies. Here are some ideas.

- Troughs placed on a balcony floor, with trailing stems and flowers cascading outwards over the floor.
- Pots, filled with brightly colored summer-flowering plants, securely fixed to the tops of decorative balustrades.
- Tubs of slightly tender plants that can be taken indoors in winter yet still give a good balcony display. Cordylines and Agaves, as well as Yuccas, are excellent plants to use.

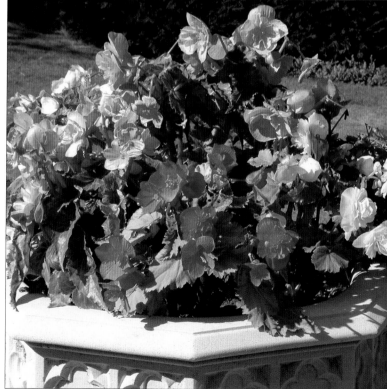

Floriferous begonias introduce a medley of bright flowers to containers throughout the summer months.

Range of containers

Many types of containers can be used, but essentially they need to hold enough compost to support plants, create a firm base, be attractive and harmonize with their surroundings. Formal containers are ideal for neat and clinical gardens, while rustic types are better for rural gardens that exude a relaxed and easy-going atmosphere. Good construction materials include wood, metal, fiberglass, plastic and reconstituted stone – and even used car tires!

What sort of container?

KEEPING COOL!

Some container materials, such as wood, are slow to warm up in summer as well as providing insulation for soil and roots during cold winters. Others, like thin plastic and metal, warm up rapidly in summer and soon heat up the soil. Fiberglass is less heat-conductive, while earthenware and reconstituted stone containers keep roots cool in summer.

CONTAINER OPTIONS

Window boxes
Several materials are used in window box construction.
- **Wood is ideal** and can be tailored to fit most windowsills, although not in excess of 2½ ft (75 cm) long. Preferably use a wooden window box as an outer container, with a 2 ft (60 cm) long, 8 in (20 cm) wide and 8 in (20 cm) deep plastic trough-like box inside it, which can be changed from one season to another.
- **Plastic window boxes** are durable if thick and rigid, but become brittle. They are therefore best used as an inner container. Strong sunlight often degrades them.
- **Terracotta has** a color and texture that harmonizes with plants. If knocked, terracotta cracks.
- **Reconstituted stone** creates an attractive feature, but is too heavy except for positioning on concrete windowsills.
- **Fiberglass** is long-lived and often used to imitate lead and other metals. If dropped, it is likely to crack.
- **Ornate-textured metal window boxes** are sometimes available. They warm up quickly in summer and are best used in conjunction with an inner plastic container.

↑ *Window boxes packed with colorful, scented plants bring color and fragrance to a house as well as a patio.*

Hanging baskets
Several materials are used to make hanging-baskets.
- **Wire-framed baskets** are popular and made in several sizes, from 10 in (25 cm) to 18 in (45 cm) wide. Most are coated in plastic to prevent corrosion and to ensure a long, attractive life.
- **Plastic hanging baskets** help to prevent soil drying out rapidly. They are available in several colors. Those with drip-tray built into their bases are ideal for positioning in lobbies and porches, where water dripping from a basket's base would be a problem. There are several designs, in various widths and depths to suit many different positions.
- **Basket lining materials** are essential for wire-framed baskets. Sphagnum moss is a traditional lining material, but now proprietary liners as well as black plastic are popular. Some liners help to conserve moisture in the basket.

↑ *Hanging baskets are a marvellous way to enjoy eye-height color all through the summer.*

Troughs
The shape and proportions of troughs roughly resemble those of window boxes, but because they are positioned on the ground troughs can be larger and so accommodate bigger plants. These decorative containers are ideal for a few culinary herbs placed near a kitchen door.
- **Fiberglass** is strong and can be given an ornate metal appearance. It is best used for relatively small troughs.
- **Reconstituted stone** troughs are often large and decorative, with an informal and relaxed surface. They are expensive to buy.
- **Wooden** troughs are good for rustic settings and are made either of planks of wood or sections of bark.
- **Terracotta** troughs are ideal for positioning at the edge of a patio or terrace, or alongside a house wall and in conjunction with pots and tubs. Terracotta containers are quite vulnerable to knocks.
- **Plastic** troughs are short-lived containers and look best when trailing stems and flowers cloak their sides.

FURTHER CONTAINER OPTIONS

Tubs, pots and urns

These have varied uses, as well as differing materials in their construction.

- **Wooden tubs** are good for relaxed and informal displays. Make sure that drainage holes are drilled in the base, and each tub stands on 3–4 bricks.
- **Versailles planters** (square, box-like containers) are usually made of wood, but some are fiberglass.
- **Jardinières** were traditionally made of lead, but nowadays these are replicated in fiberglass.
- **Concrete containers**, perhaps shallow and cone-shaped, are popular but are not suitable for rustic settings. Because their sides and base are thick, they are difficult to move.
- **Earthenware pots** and tubs have a natural appearance and are ideal for many types of plant.
- **Reconstituted stone urns** are distinctive and ideal for summer flowers and other seasonal plants.

Cut-out planters

Some containers have cupped openings in their sides in which plants such as herbs, strawberries and bulbs can be planted. Many home-constructed containers, such as small barrels with windows cut in their sides, are ideal for summer-flowering plants or even longer-lived types such as *Sempervivum* (Houseleeks), which produce masses of evergreen rosettes.

Good drainage is essential in these containers, especially for herbs and strawberries that remain in the container for several years.

↑ *Strawberries grown in planters look good, and taste better than bought ones.*

↑ *For an original display, use a small barrel with a window cut out of one side.*

Found items

Many attics and garden sheds harbor attractive artefacts that can be dusted off and used as containers for plants. These range from metal teapots and kettles to discarded watering-cans and old chimney pots. Some of these can be used alone, while others look good when modified with another container.

← *Plants in small and decorative containers need regular care.*
→ *Try mixing-and-matching containers by placing a hanging basket on top of a wide, old chimney pot.*

GROWING-BAGS ON PATIOS

Growing-bags are inexpensive to buy yet are able to bring masses of color and interest to patios.

- **Grow tomatoes** in growing-bags, using bamboo canes or proprietary structures to support the plants.
- **Plant growing-bags in autumn** with spring-flowering bulbs. It is possible to reuse growing-bags earlier used for tomatoes; top up with peat.
- **Place growing-bags** with trailing summer-flowering bedding plants along the edges of flat-roofed garages.

MINIATURE WATER GARDENS IN CONTAINERS

An old, deep, stone sink enables the creation of a miniature water garden on a patio. Wooden tubs can also be used. Include only miniature water plants.

Miniature water gardens are ideal for patios and small gardens.

Small containers are summer-only homes for miniature water plants. Move them into a greenhouse or conservatory in winter.

Range of plants for containers

Which plants suit containers?

Good plants for containers range from summer- and spring-flowering bedding plants to small shrubs, trees and conifers. Bamboos, as well as herbs, vegetables and fruit, are other possibilities. Small alpine plants in stone sinks create choice features, as well as miniature water plants in tubs or deep stone sinks. Displayed on these pages is a parade of plants for growing in containers, many of which are sure to capture your imagination.

GROWING PLANTS IN CONTAINERS

The central problem in growing plants in containers is the limited amount of soil available to them to create stability as well as supplying water and nutrients. Additionally, because containers are exposed and, perhaps, positioned on windowsills, at the edges of balconies and on tops of walls, they are vulnerable to buffeting wind, strong sunlight during summer and freezing weather in winter. Nevertheless, container-gardening enthusiasts never fail to reveal dedication to their art and invariably clothe their gardens in color throughout the year. It is also an ideal way to grow plants in small gardens.

FRUIT IN CONTAINERS

Strawberries in barrels or strawberry pots are popular – they are easy to grow and the same plants will produce fruits over several years. Apples grown on dwarfing rootstocks, such as M27 and M9, can be grown in large pots.

Summer-flowering bedding plants

These are widely grown during summer in pots, tubs, troughs, window boxes and hanging baskets.

- It is possible to raise plants yourself from seeds sown in gentle warmth in late winter or early spring, then grown and slowly acclimatized to outdoor conditions for planting in late spring or early summer (depending on the weather and your area).

- It is also possible to buy young plants and to plant them directly into containers.

Hardy border plants

These plants can be left in tubs or large pots for several years until congested and need to be removed and divided.

- Some of these plants are herbaceous, and others retain some or all of their leaves throughout the winter.

- Buy healthy, well-established plants and, preferably, plant them in spring or early summer.

- Border plants such as Hostas, which are vulnerable to slugs and snails, are given slight protection from these pests.

Small shrubs

Both flowering and foliage shrubs can be grown in tubs and large pots. Later, they can be moved into a garden.

- Flowering shrubs are seasonal and, while some flower in spring, others have flowers in summer.

- Evergreen shrubs – especially the variegated types – create attractive features right through the year.

- Architectural shrubs, such as Yuccas, are ideal for a Mediterranean garden or for a formal one where sharp, clinical lines are desired.

Small trees

Small trees are possible candidates for tubs, especially if low-growing and not creating a major barrier for strong wind in winter, when their roots could be rocked and loosened in the soil.

- The beautiful deciduous shrub *Acer palmatum* 'Dissectum Atropurpureum' forms a low canopy of deeply dissected, bronze-red leaves throughout summer.

- *Acer palmatum* 'Dissectum' is closely related and similarly shaped, with finely dissected green leaves.

Bulbs

Winter-, spring- and early-summer-flowering bulbs are ideal for containers. With their reserve of food, bulbs are some of nature's best-equipped plants for creating color.

- Miniature winter- and spring-flowering types are best reserved for planting in sink gardens, where they combine well with small rock-garden plants.

- Early spring-flowering bulbs such as Daffodils burst into life and drench containers with color.

Herbs

Many culinary herbs can be grown in containers. While Bay, with its tall and stately appearance, is ideal for tubs or large pots, small herbs are better in pots and planters.

- Try a medley of Chives, Thyme and Sage in a planter with cupped holes in its sides.

- Plant Mint in individual pots in order to constrain its invasive nature.

- Sow Parsley in small, ornate containers that will perfectly set off the densely curled, mid-green leaves.

Climbers

Climbers introduce vertical color – some live for only one year while others survive from one year to another.

- Plant a large-flowered Clematis in a large pot and let it spread over ornate railings.

- Plant young Sweet Pea plants in large pots in early summer – they will create color throughout the summer.

- Plant a tub with *Humulus lupulus* 'Aureus' (Yellow-leaved Hop); support it with a 5 ft (1.5 m) high trellis of garden canes.

Bamboos

Several bamboos are ideal for planting in tubs or large pots. They are superb for positioning in a Japanese garden.

- Plant small bamboos in large pots and taller ones in wooden tubs or square boxes.

- Stand the container out of direct sunlight and away from strong drafts.

- When plants become congested, in late spring either repot into a larger container or remove, divide and repot into 2–3 pots.

Vegetables

Many vegetables that have fibrous or shallow roots can be grown successfully in containers.

- New potatoes are possible in large pots and growing-bags. Proprietary potato-growing containers are available.

- Tomatoes are popular for planting in pots and positioning on a warm, sheltered patio.

- Lettuces are ideal for growing in growing-bags and placing on a patio – but only where slugs and snails cannot reach them.

Water-garden plants

These can be created in tubs or deep, stone sinks. Wooden tubs are better than stone sinks as they insulate the water from temperature extremes.

- Miniature, non-invasive aquatic plants are ideal and these include *Carex elata* 'Aurea' (also known as *Carex stricta* 'Bowles Golden'), *Typha minima* and *Schoenoplectus lacustris* subsp. *tabernaemontani* 'Zebrinus' (also known as *Scirpus zebrinus* and commonly as Zebra Rush) with quill-like stems banded in white and green.

Vestibules and porches

Vestibules and porches are ideal for the hardier houseplants and many are superb when planted in hanging baskets. However, none of them will survive frost-like conditions.

- There are several suitable fern-like houseplants for this purpose, such as *Asplenium bulbiferum* (Mother Fern) and *Asparagus densiflorus* (Asparagus Fern).

- The flowering *Campanula isophylla* (Star of Bethlehem) is moderately hardy, with star-shaped blue flowers in summer.

Dwarf conifers

Dwarf and slow-growing conifers are ideal for creating shape and color interest throughout the year, whether in tubs or large pots, or grouped together in a large trough.

- Position conifers out of strong, direct or blustery wind, which is a danger to them.

- In windy areas, plant conifers in heavy containers that give them a firm base – and use loam-based potting soil.

- Make sure the potting soil is neither too dry in summer nor too wet in winter.

Positioning and using containers

Where should I place containers?

Some containers can be put in many different and imaginative positions on a patio, around a house or in a garden. They can be used to highlight features such as patio windows, porches and flights of steps, as well as directing foot traffic away from open casement windows. They are also ideal for creating focal points within a garden. Window boxes are dedicated solely to windowsills, but they are still an essential part of the art of container gardening.

WINDOW BOXES FOR ALL SEASONS

Window boxes are superb for brightening windows throughout the year. As soon as a spring display ends, a summer-flowering one can be put in its place. When, in autumn, that fades, a winter display can be ready to take its place. Positioning window boxes needs care. For sash windows (where two frameworks of glass are raised and lowered vertically) a window box can be placed on the sill. For casement windows (which are hinged at their outer edges and open over the sill) window boxes are best placed on strong brackets attached below the window.

Tubs and pots

Groups of tubs and pots create attractive features on patios and terraces, either grouped in small clusters in a sheltered corner or near a patio or kitchen door.

- **When in small groups**, plants afford each other slight protection from strong, gusty winds, as well as creating a mini-environment that is slightly more humid.

- **By using pots** singly or in small groups, the tops of flights of steps can be made more decorative. Use low plants at the top, and taller ones (perhaps upright conifers with colorful foliage) at the base.

Troughs

Troughs are versatile containers and create captivating displays on their own or with groups of pots.

- **Small troughs are ideal** for brightening the edges of patios at ground level or, with the aid of metal supports, fitted to the tops of balustrades.

- **A decorative trough**, with a pot on either side burgeoning with flowers, looks good when placed in front of a window. Leave space between the window and the trough, so that watering and maintenance can be carried out easily.

Wall baskets

Wall baskets create magnificent display containers against walls. Wire-framed wall baskets come in a variety of shapes and sizes. Choose a style, shape and size appropriate to the architecture it will be hung on.

- **Wall baskets** are excellent for positioning under windows, while small ones are better on walls that are bare and need brightening.

- **Use wall baskets** in combinations with troughs and plants in pots.

- **Position wall baskets** on balcony walls, perhaps on either side of a door. Ensure the door opens freely.

Tubs

Tubs, as well as square and box-like containers, are ideal for shrubs and small trees. They create eye-catching features.

- **Use two large containers** and plant a half-standard *Laurus nobilis* (Bay) tree in each of them. Position them on either side of an entrance. Full standard trees can be used, but usually they are too dominant and certainly more susceptible to damage from strong wind.

- **Round tubs** offer informality and are suitable for a dome-topped shrub or small tree.

Miniature water gardens

Position miniature water gardens in slight or variable shade to ensure that the water does not become excessively warm. Also, avoid overhanging trees.

- **Position the water feature** where it can be easily looked after each day. At the height of summer the water will require regular topping up to compensate for evaporation.

- **A grouping of** a miniature water garden and an old, shallow, stone sink planted with small rock-garden plants and miniature bulbs never fails to attract attention from passers-by.

- **Adding a small fountain** to keep the water moving will reduce the likelihood of mosquitoes breeding in the water.

Grow bags

Grow bags are more versatile and economical than most other containers – although not always as pleasing to the eye.

- **Tomatoes, lettuces** and other vegetables are popular candidates for grow bags. Position them in good light, with shelter from cold winds in early summer.

- **Plant them with** low-growing culinary herbs and place them near a kitchen door.

- **To produce flowers** for indoor decoration, plant with self-supporting bedding plants. Set in an out-of-the-way spot.

Herb pots and planters

Herb planters are ideal for positioning on patios and near kitchen doors. Herbs can also be grown in pots, and these are best displayed in small clusters or in combination with the herb planter.

- **Herb planters**, with their informal appearance, are ideal for rustic patios perhaps surfaced with old stone slabs and with gaps left between them for small plants such as Thyme.

- **Try positioning** a herb planter on a paving slab at the end of a flower border.

Hanging baskets

Hanging baskets are versatile and can be used in many exciting and colorful ways. Here are a few display situations to consider.

- **Use two baskets** on either side of a window. Position them so that the edges of the display slightly intrude on the window frame.

- **Suspend a few** hanging baskets along the edge of a veranda.

- **The ends of carports** benefit from color, but ensure that you will not bump into the baskets.

- **Dull and bland courtyard walls** are soon brightened by the addition of a hanging basket.

Sink gardens

Shallow stone sinks have an informal presence that harmonizes with relaxed and cottage-garden settings.

- **If you have several** sink gardens, position them at different heights. Four pillars of ornate but structurally sound bricks will make plants easier to admire – and look after.

- **Gardeners in wheelchairs** appreciate raised but stable sink gardens.

- **A sink garden** can be positioned to direct foot traffic, perhaps away from the corner of a building or a window.

Wheelbarrows

When drenched with brightly colored, summer-flowering plants, a wheelbarrow can become a center of attention – a focal point for a patio or a front garden.

- **Always put a wheelbarrow** in place before filling it with plants. When full of potting soil and plants – and well watered – the weight may prevent the barrow being safely moved without the risk of it collapsing.

- **Position the barrow** with its front end attractively angled towards the main viewing area.

Seasonal displays

Color through the year?

By using seasonal arrangements of plants in window boxes it is possible to create color throughout the year. Hanging baskets are mostly used for displays in summer, while wall baskets are ideal for both spring and summer. Tubs usually hold perennial plants such as small shrubs, trees and conifers, and these remain attractive for several years. Sink gardens are best in spring and early summer, and miniature water gardens throughout summer.

GETTING THE MOST COLOR AND INTEREST

The smaller the garden, the more difficult it is to create interest in borders throughout the year. However, by using containers it is possible to produce color in every season, including winter.

Window boxes can have a yearly cycle of three different seasonal displays, so they are superb for outdoor viewing as well as from indoors. See page 53 for the philosophy of using window boxes in this way.

Hanging baskets displayed outdoors bring only summer color, but when planted with resilient indoor plants can be placed in a vestibule or porch for year-round interest.

Wall baskets and troughs can be planted with bulbs and biennial plants in autumn and, when the display is over in late spring or early summer, replanted with summer-flowering bedding plants.

SEASONS

Throughout this book, advice is given about seasonal tasks. Because of global and even regional variations in climate and temperature (even within a distance of 100 miles / 160 km, the arrival of spring can vary by a week or more), the four main seasons have been used, with each subdivided into "early," "mid-" and "late" – for example, early spring, mid-spring and late spring. These 12 divisions of the year can be applied to the appropriate calendar months in your local area, if you find this helps.

SPRING DISPLAYS

Window boxes

The range of spring-flowering plants – from bulbs to hardy biennials – is wide. Here are two arrangements that create exciting displays.

Medley display (biennials and bulbs): double *Bellis perennis* (Daisy), *Myosotis* (Forget-me-not), *Muscari armeniacum* (Grape Hyacinth), *Tulipa greigii* (Species Tulip), *Tulipa fosteriana* (Species Tulip) and *Erysimum cheiri* (Wallflower).

Medley display (mainly bulbs, plus Polyanthus): *Hyacinthus orientalis* (Hyacinth), *Iris danfordiae* and *Iris reticulata* (Miniature Irises), *Narcissus* (Miniature Trumpet Daffodils), *Primula polyantha* (Polyanthus) and *Tulipa greigii* (Species Tulip).

Color in troughs

Troughs positioned at ground level and in a wind-sheltered position near to a house or patio wall are ideal for Trumpet-Flowered Daffodils in spring. However, if exposed to blustery spring wind, the flowers and stems can soon be damaged. A trough that can be seen and admired from kitchen or living-room windows is a bonus.

Color in tubs

Tubs are more suitable than troughs for dominant displays in spring. In autumn, plant a mixture of Single Early Tulips and Hyacinths. The Tulips grow 12–15 in (30–38 cm) high and in a wide color range. Hyacinths are shorter and in colors that include white, pink, red and blue. For extra color and to soften the tub's sides, plant variegated small-leaved Ivies around the edges.

Grow bags

In autumn, after growing a few tomato plants, remove all plant debris, top up with moist peat and plant a selection of spring-flowering bulbs. Water well and place the grow bag in a cool area. In spring the bulbs will burst into flower.

SUMMER DISPLAYS

Hanging baskets

To many container-gardening enthusiasts, hanging baskets are the best way to introduce summer color on a patio and around a house. As they create color at eye height, any blemishes that arise throughout the summer are soon noticed. Here are a few tips:

- Don't cram in too many plants. Once established, fewer but bigger and healthier plants will look better than masses of starved plants.
- Don't use too many different types of plant. A basket planted with a dozen different plants will not look as effective as 12 plants of only 4–5 different kinds.

Window boxes

The range of plants for summer-flowering window boxes is wide; some are upright and bushy, while others trail and help to cloak the sides of the container. Here are two medleys of plants to consider.

Medley display (mainly flowers): summer-flowering *Viola* x *wittrockiana* (Pansies), *Lobularia maritima* (Sweet Alyssum; also known as *Alyssum maritimum*), *Lobelia erinus* (Trailing Lobelia), *Begonia* x *tuberhybrida* (Tuberous-Rooted Begonia) and Zonal Pelargonium.

Medley display (flowers and foliage): *Bassia scoparia* 'Trichophylla' (Burning Bush; also known as *Kochia scoparia* 'Trichophylla'), *Impatiens* (Busy Lizzie), Godetia, *Lysimachia nummularia* (Creeping Jenny) and *Lobelia erinus* (Trailing Lobelia).

↑ *A combination of bushy and trailing plants is essential in a well-balanced box.*

Decorative pots

↑ *Fancy pots in a mixture of sizes and shapes create exciting features on patios and terraces. Some can have a single-color theme, and others a medley of hues. Baskets with a plant pot inside introduce a rural variation to the display.*

WINTER DISPLAYS

Window boxes

Winter displays in window boxes mainly rely on small evergreen shrubs, with variegated trailing plants to soften the edges of the box. Some shrubs, when small, are used for one season and later planted into a larger tub or garden. Because winter-flowering window boxes are usually replanted each autumn, it is an opportunity to try a wide range of plants. Here are a few types to consider. **Berried shrubs:** choose small, heavily berried plants. **Dwarf conifers:** the range is wide and in many attractive colors. **Evergreen shrubs:** these range from the variegated *Aucuba japonica* 'Variegata' to all-green types such as *Gaultheria procumbens*. **Flowering shrubs:** these are more limited than evergreen types, but include winter-flowering *Erica* (Heathers). **Hedera helix (small-leaved variegated Ivies):** many colorful varieties are available.

Tubs

→ Juniperus horizontalis 'Wiltonii' (Wilton Carpet Juniper) is slow-growing and carpet-forming, 6–8 in (15–20 cm) high and spreading to about 3½ ft (1 m) wide in six years. However, when small it creates an attractive feature with its bright blue, dense foliage. It needs a wide container, such as a tub, so that it can spread.

← Chamaecyparis lawsoniana 'Elwoodii' is a slow-growing conifer that eventually reaches 6 ft (1.8 m) high, but when small is ideal for planting in a window box. It is packed with dark green leaves. An alternative is 'Ellwood's Golden Pillar,' with golden-yellow foliage.

← Several Skimmias have berries that persist into winter. Their bright berries create further variation in a pot on a patio. Position them towards the center of the container to give them protection from birds, which soon decimate plants.

Contrasts and harmonies

Producing attractive color harmonies and contrasts is just a matter of selecting plants that suit their backgrounds. On this page is suggested a wide range of plants that will suit white, gray-stone, red-brick or dark walls, in both spring and summer seasons. Some of these displays create striking contrasts that soon capture people's attention, while others produce warm and subtle harmonies between plants and their background.

How do I create good color combinations?

INFLUENCE OF GREEN

Green is the most common color in a garden and the surface texture of a leaf strongly influences its perceived color.
- A smooth-surfaced leaf reflects light at the same angle at which the light hits it, making the light purer in color than the same light reflected from a matte surface.
- In nature, few plant surfaces are as smooth as glass, and the scattering of reflected light occurs on the surfaces of most leaves.

CHANGING LIGHT

Throughout the day the intensity of light varies, influencing its perception.

- Pale colors are the first to become discernible in the morning light, as well as the last to be seen in the evening and at dusk.
- Conversely, dark colors such as dark reds and purples are usually the last colors to be seen in the morning, and the first to fade at dusk.

Light, bright colors remain noticeable even into the late evening.

WHITE BACKGROUNDS

Spring displays

White backgrounds are ideal for highlighting yellow, gold, red, scarlet and dark blue flowers, as well as green foliage which acts as a neutral color. Choose combinations such as: • *Myosotis* (Forget-me-nots) and golden *Erysimum cheiri* (Wallflowers; also known as *Cheiranthus cheiri*). • Double *Bellis perennis* (Daisies) and red Wallflowers. • Blue and red *Hyacinthus orientalis* (Hyacinths) and spring-flowering Crocuses, such as the large-flowered hybrids of *Crocus chrysanthus*.

Summer displays

The range of color-contrasting displays is larger in summer than in spring. Choose combinations such as:
• Golden-faced *Tagetes* (Marigolds), dark red *Pelargonium* (Geraniums) and yellow Zinnias. Add the tender *Asparagus densiflorus* 'Sprengeri' (Emerald Fern) to the display.
• Trailing red-flowered *Tropaeolum majus* (Nasturtiums) and yellow *Calceolaria* x *herbeohybrida* (Slipper Flower) with its pouch-like flowers. Add copious amounts of *Asparagus densiflorus* (Asparagus Fern).

GRAY-STONE BACKGROUNDS

Spring displays

Gray-stone walls enhance and highlight pinks, reds, deep blues and purples. Choose combinations such as:
• For positions in full sun, completely plant the container with red, crimson and purple or scarlet *Erysimum cheiri* (Wallflowers; also known as *Cheiranthus cheiri*). • Deep blue *Myosotis* (Forget-me-nots) and pink or blue *Hyacinthus orientalis* (Hyacinths). • For a distinctive and clinically shaped display, use just blue *Hyacinthus orientalis* (Hyacinths).

Summer displays

There are many superb flowers that will create distinctive displays. Choose combinations such as: • A medley of deep blue *Lobelia erinus* (Lobelia) and scarlet *Pelargonium* (Geraniums). • Blue-flowered *Campanula isophylla* (Star of Bethlehem) and blue *Matthiola incana* (Stocks). • A mixture of Petunias, *Campanula isophylla* (Star of Bethlehem), pink-flowered ivy-leaved *Pelargonium* (Geraniums) and dark red *Pelargonium* (Geraniums).

RED-BRICK BACKGROUNDS

Spring displays

Red-brick walls create color-dominant backgrounds that can overwhelm plants unless used in large clusters. Select plants with white, soft blue, silver and lemon flowers. Silver-leaved plants are also highlighted by red-brick walls. Choose combinations such as: • Light blue *Myosotis* (Forget-me-nots) and white *Hyacinthus orientalis* (Hyacinths). • Bronze and cream *Erysimum cheiri* (Wallflowers; also known as *Cheiranthus cheiri*) and double, white *Bellis perennis* (Daisies).

Summer displays

There are many superb flowers to choose from to create colorful and distinctive displays. Choose combinations such as: • For sunny positions, use a medley of white *Chrysanthemum frutescens* (Marguerites; also known as *Argyranthemum frutescens*), soft-blue Stocks, trailing Lobelia and the silver-foliaged *Senecio cineraria*. • *Lobularia maritima* (Sweet Alyssum; also known as *Alyssum maritimum*), soft blue Stocks and the silver-foliaged *Senecio cineraria*.

DARK BACKGROUNDS

Spring displays

Dark backgrounds create strong contrasts for bright and light colors, and are stronger than those produced against red-brick backgrounds. Choose combinations such as: • A dense medley of white or yellow *Hyacinthus orientalis* (Hyacinths). • A strong duo of white *Hyacinthus orientalis* (Hyacinths) and yellow *Crocus chrysanthus* (Crocuses). For added color and to soften the edges of the container, plant variegated small-leaved *Hedera helix* (Ivies).

Summer displays

During summer, there are more plants for creating dramatic contrasts. Choose combinations such as: • Position the yellow-flowered and trailing *Lysimachia nummularia* (Creeping Jenny) close to the edges of the container, with the yellow-flowered *Calceolaria* x *herbeohybrida* (Slipper Flower) and dramatically yellow varieties of the tuberous-rooted *Begonia* x *tuberhybrida*. For extra color, use the yellow-leaved form of Creeping Jenny.

WALL BASKETS

Red and yellow flowers contrast well against white walls.

Pink, red, deep blue and purple flowers are ideal for gray-stone walls.

White and blue flowers are highlighted by red-brick walls.

Wall baskets are secured to walls and therefore make contrasts and harmonies between backgrounds and plants readily apparent. Here are a few combinations of plants to consider. **For positioning against white walls:** Use yellow, gold, red, scarlet and dark blue flowers, as well as green foliage. • Combination of Zinnias, *Pelargonium* (Geraniums) and *Asparagus densiflorus* 'Sprengeri' (Emerald Fern). • Emerald Fern, bright yellow *Calceolaria* x *herbeohybrida* (Slipper Flowers) and trailing red Nasturtiums. **For positioning against gray-stone walls:** Use pink, red, deep blue and purple flowers. • Blue-flowered *Campanula isophylla* (Star of Bethlehem), Petunias and *Pelargonium* (Geraniums). • Cascading red or pink Fuchsia, trailing Begonias and an edging of a variegated *Helichrysum petiolare* (Licorice Plant). **For positioning against red-brick walls:** Use white, soft blue, silver and lemon flowers, and silver foliage. • White Tulips, blue-flowered *Muscari armeniacum* (Grape Hyacinths) and variegated small-leaved *Hedera helix* (Ivies). • White *Chrysanthemum frutescens* (Marguerites; also known as *Argyranthemum frutescens*), soft blue trailing Lobelias and blue *Matthiola incana* (Stocks).

INFLUENCE OF COLOR

Blue is associated with calmness and is said to lower blood pressure and to slow up the breathing and pulse rate. A garden that needs to promote a sense of tranquillity should be predominantly blue – but not a dark shade.

Yellow is the color of brightness and cheerfulness and is claimed to be the primary color of the intellect, hope and productivity. Therefore, for a garden that imparts originality of thought and vitality, select yellow-flowered or yellow-leaved plants.

Red is an emotional color and, in contrast to blue, is said to raise blood pressure and increase the rate of respiration. It is also the color of sexual invitation and this, no doubt, accounts for an increased pulse rate.

Green is nature's unifying color and introduces a cool and soothing ambience. It is ideal as a background for other colors and, in containers, to highlight demure shades and suffuse strong colors.

Creating a scented patio

Are there many different fragrances?

The range of fragrances that can be introduced into a garden and containers is wide and includes those as diverse as new-mown hay, parsley, resin, violets, honey, myrrh and jasmine. However, not all of these fragrances will be produced by plants growing in containers on a patio, and it is possible to add to their scents by planting fragrant climbers in soil alongside a patio and training them over a trellis or against a house wall.

POSITIONING SCENTED CONTAINERS

Containers with scented plants, and when grouped on a warm, sheltered patio, produce concentrated areas of fragrance. Most flowers readily release their fragrance, but some conifers have aromatic foliage that needs to be gently rubbed for it to become apparent. Many small conifers for containers have unusual fragrances, ranging from resinous to warm and sweet. However, some of their scents are reminiscent of soap and paint.

Fragrance in some flowers is immediately noticeable, while for others, such as some Violets, it is initially apparent but after only a few moments disappears completely. Then later it can again be detected. This is only the nose playing tricks.

Hanging baskets

Hanging baskets have a limited amount of soil and therefore are best used solely for summer-flowering plants. Nevertheless, there are opportunities to create memorable fragrances.

- *Lobularia maritima*, trailing variety (Sweet Alyssum; also known as *Alyssum maritimum*): new-mown hay redolence. The flowers attract bees, so put the basket where bees will not be a problem.
- Trailing *Tropaeolum majus* (Nasturtiums): faintly scented flowers, with leaves that, when bruised, emit pungency.

Window boxes

There are many plants that create fragrance in window boxes, ranging from small bulbs to miniature conifers and summer bedding plants.

Bulbs:
- *Crocus chrysanthus* (Crocus): sweet.
- *Hyacinthus orientalis* (Hyacinth): strongly sweet.
- *Iris danfordiae*: honey-scented.
- *Iris reticulata*: violet-scented.

Summer-flowering bedding plants:
- Flowering *Nicotiana* (Tobacco Plant): richly sweet.
- *Heliotropium arborescens* (Heliotrope): cherry pie.
- *Viola* x *wittrockiana* (Pansies): cool and slightly sweet.
- *Lobularia maritima* (Sweet Alyssum; also known as *Alyssum maritimum*): new-mown hay.

Plants in pots

The range of scented plants for tubs is wide and ranges from shrubs to Lilies. Additionally, small conifers can also be used. Some of these plants can also be grown in large pots.

Shrubs:
- *Buxus sempervirens* 'Elegantissima' (Box): pale green, honey-scented flowers.
- *Santolina chamaecyparissus* (Cotton Lavender): chamomile fragrant foliage.
- *Rosmarinus officinalis* (Rosemary): rosemary-scented leaves.
- *Salvia officinalis* (Sage): sage-scented leaves.

Wall baskets

Wall baskets are ideal for creating centers of strong fragrance, especially from summer-flowering bedding plants (see "Window boxes" opposite). Although fragrant miniature bulbs can be planted in autumn, this often means removing summer-flowering displays before they have completed their full display. If, however, this is not a problem, plant a medley of miniature bulbs, as well as bold and very sweet *Hyacinthus orientalis* (Hyacinths). These are available in several colors, but it is the white ones that usually have the strongest fragrance. Because displays in wall baskets are regularly changed, miniature and slow-growing conifers are not suitable.

Climbers

Some fragrant climbers can be planted in tubs and large pots and these include the popular Lathyrus odoratus *(Sweet Pea). Fresh plants are raised each year. Other climbers are better suited for planting at the edge of a patio and training against a trellis. Some of these have unusual fragrances, including:*

- *Clematis flammula*: hawthorn-scented.
- *Jasminum officinale*: jasmine-scented.
- *Lonicera americana*: honey-scented.
- *Wisteria*: vanilla-scented.

Troughs

Small troughs that are positioned at ground level can be treated in the same way as window boxes. They are also ideal for planting dwarf and slow-growing conifers. Large troughs can be planted or sown with a wide range of plants, including Night-scented Stocks and Virginian Stocks (see below). Many Stocks have superb fragrances, including forms of *Matthiola incana*. They are clove-scented and have given rise to Perpetual-flowering Stocks, Brompton Stocks, Ten-week Stocks and East Lothian Stocks.

EVENING AND NIGHT SCENTS

Where there is space under a window and between a patio, this is ideal for a color and fragrance-packed combination of *Matthiola bicornis* (Night-scented Stock) and *Malcolmia maritima* (Virginian Stock). They are ideal companions – the Night-scented Stock provides the fragrance, but has an untidy nature, while the Virginian Stock with its red, lilac, rose or white flowers provides color. Both are hardy annuals and therefore they can be raised very easily.

- **Night-scented Stock:** sow seeds ¼ in (6 mm) deep from early to late spring, where they are to flower. Thin the seedlings to 6–9 in (15–23 cm) apart.
- **Virginian Stock:** sow seeds ¼ in (6 mm) deep from early to late spring, where they are to flower. Thin seedlings to 6 in (15 cm) apart; plants flower about four weeks after being sown and continue in bloom for up to eight weeks.

Plants in tubs

Many small, scented plants, including Lilies and dwarf conifers, can be grown in tubs on a patio.

Lilies:
- *Lilium auratum* (Golden-rayed Lily): brilliant white and sweetly fragrant.
- *Lilium longiflorum* (Easter Lily): white flowers with a honey-like scent.

Dwarf and slow-growing conifers:
- *Juniperus virginiana* (Pencil Cedar): soap and paint redolence.
- *Chamaecyparis obtusa* (Hinoki Cypress): warm and sweet redolence.
- *Chamaecyparis pisifera* (Sawara Cypress): resin-like fragrance.

ROSE FRAGRANCES

Several fragrant Roses are ideal for planting alongside a patio to introduce further scents. These include:

- 'Blush Noisette': clove-like scent (Climber).
- 'Constance Spry': myrrh-scented (Shrub Rose or Climber).
- 'The Garland': orange-like scent (Rambler).
- 'Leander': fruity scent (Shrub Rose or Climber).
- 'René André': apple-like scent (Rambler).
- 'Paul Transon': apple-like scent (Rambler).

Summer-flowering bedding plants

Summer-flowering bedding plants are usually half-hardy annuals that are raised in gentle warmth in late winter or early spring, and later, when all risk of frost has passed, planted into containers. Their range is wide, both in color and in style of growth. Some are bushy, whereas others have a cascading or trailing habit that helps to unify the display and soften the edges of containers, especially hanging baskets and window boxes.

How do I grow these plants?

SUMMER-FLOWERING AND FOLIAGE PLANTS

In addition to the many summer-flowering seed-raised bedding plants, there are those grown for their beautiful leaves that help to create greater eye appeal and to highlight flowering types. These include the silver-leaved *Senecio cineraria* 'Silver Dust,' *Helichrysum petiolare* (Licorice Plant) and its many variegated and colored-leaf forms, and the yellow-leaved form of *Lysimachia nummularia* 'Aurea' (Creeping Jenny). Other attractively leaved plants include *Pelargonium peltatum* (Ivy-leaved Geraniums) and Zonal Pelargoniums, both of which have the bonus of flowers.

WHEN TO PLANT ...

Half-hardy plants are soon damaged by late spring frost, and therefore are best not planted until all risk of low temperatures has passed. Clearly, this much depends on the area and its vulnerability to late frost, but increasingly the climate is becoming warmer and containers can be planted earlier than several decades ago.

Vulnerable positions:
• Cold, shaded aspects.
• Low-lying positions, perhaps at the base of a slope and where cold air collects.
• At the corners of buildings, where cold air is channelled from one position to another.

Ageratum houstonianum
Floss Flower (USA/UK)
Pussy-foot (USA)
Height: 5–12 in (13–30 cm)
Spread: 6–12 in (15–30 cm)
Half-hardy annual, with bluish-mauve flowers. There are many varieties, in bright blue, mauve, pink and white.

Anagallis monelli
Blue Pimpernel (USA/UK)
Height: 9 in (23 cm)
Spread: 9 in (23 cm)
Half-hardy annual with a neat, compact habit and masses of large, azure-blue flowers from spring to autumn.

Asarina purpusii 'Victoria Falls'
Height: 5–6 in (13–15 cm)
Spread: 6–8 in (15–20 cm)
Half-hardy annual with a tumbling mass of cerise-purple flowers with long trumpets. Trails up to 15 in (38 cm).

Asarina x hybrida 'Red Dragon'
Climbing, ideal for baskets, where stems can be supported.
Half-hardy annual, with carmine-red flowers, up to 3 in (7.5 cm) long. Plants become drenched in color.

Begonia semperflorens 'Stara Mixed'
Fibrous Begonia (UK)
Wax Begonia (USA/UK)
Height: 8–10 in (20–25 cm)
Spread: 10–12 in (25–30 cm)
Half-hardy, branching annual with flowers in white, rose and scarlet.

Begonia sutherlandii 'Orange Shower'

Trailing

Half-hardy, tuberous-rooted begonia with a cascading nature. Distinctive orange flowers. Ideal for planting in hanging baskets and wall baskets.

Begonia x tuberhybrida 'Dragon Wing'

Trailing and bushy

Half-hardy, tuberous-rooted begonia with a cascading nature. Clusters of scarlet-red flowers. Ideal for baskets and containers.

Bidens ferulifera 'Golden Eye'

Height: 8–12 in (20–25 cm)

Prostrate and tumbling

Half-hardy annual with beautiful bright yellow flowers that are borne amid fern-like foliage.

Calceolaria integrifolia 'Sunshine'

Pouch Flower (USA/UK)

Slipper Flower (USA/UK)

Height: 10–15 in (25–38 cm)

Trailing and cascading

Half-hardy shrubby perennial, ideal in a hanging basket, with yellow flowers.

Calendula officinalis

English Marigold (UK)

Pot Marigold (USA/UK)

Height: 12–15 in (30–38 cm)

Spread: 10–12 in (25–30 cm)

Hardy annual, often grown in pots, with large, daisy-like, bright yellow or orange flowers. Some forms are dwarf.

Campanula isophylla

Italian Bellflower (USA/UK)

Star of Bethlehem (USA/UK)

Height: 6 in (15 cm)

Trailing

Hardy perennial, with masses of star-shaped, 1 in (2.5 cm) wide, blue or white flowers.

Cascade Geraniums

(also known as Balcon and Continental Geraniums)

Height: 8–12 in (20–30 cm)

Trailing and cascading

Half-hardy annuals which become swamped with masses of flowers in shades of scarlet, salmon, pink and lilac.

Clematis tangutica 'Radar Love'

Height: 1½–2 ft (45–60 cm)

Climbing and scrambling

Hardy perennial, raised from seed and flowers three months after sowing. Nodding, rich yellow flowers. Ideal for hanging baskets.

WHITE AND SILVER THEMES

White- and silver-themed displays have a delicate and demure quality, especially when seen in partial shade.

• When positioned in full sun, a white and silver display becomes more intense and dramatic.

• Flowers in small, clustered heads reflect less light than large ones, and consequently look less dramatic and intensely white.

• In hot countries, where strong sunshine is assured, a white display can be too intense. Therefore, add pale mauve and faintly blue-tinged flowers to reduce the visual strength of the display.

THOMPSON & MORGAN

Datura 'Ballerina Mixed'
Thorn Apple (USA/UK)
Height: 1½–2 ft (45–60 cm)
Spread: 1½–2 ft (45–60 cm)
Half-hardy shrub raised from seeds, with upward-facing, primrose-yellow flowers flushed purple or pure white.

THOMPSON & MORGAN

Datura meteloides 'Evening Fragrance'
Thorn Apple (USA/UK)
Height: 14–18 in (35–45 cm)
Spread: 14–15 in (35–38 cm)
Half-hardy annual that bears large, trumpet-shaped, white and soft lavender, fragrant flowers.

THOMPSON & MORGAN

Eschscholzia maritima prostrata 'Golden Tears'
Californian Poppy (USA/UK)
Height: 6–9 in (15–23 cm)
Spreading and trailing to 2 ft (60 cm)
Hardy annual, usually raised as a half-hardy annual, with golden-yellow flowers amid blue-green leaves.

Heliotropium arborescens
(syn. *Heliotropium x hybridum*)
Cherry Pie (UK) **Heliotrope** (USA/UK)
Height: 15–18 in (38–45 cm)
Spread: 12–15 in (30–38 cm)
Half-hardy perennial grown as a half-hardy annual. Fragrant flowers in violet, through lavender, to white.

THOMPSON & MORGAN

Impatiens hawkererii New Guinea 'Java Flames Mixed'
Height: 9–12 in (23–30 cm)
Spread: 9–12 in (23–30 cm)
Half-hardy annual with a compact nature and masses of fluorescent flowers. Ideal for hanging baskets and other containers.

THOMPSON & MORGAN

Impatiens walleriana 'Unique'
Busy Lizzie (USA/UK)
Height: 8–10 in (20–25 cm)
Spread: 8–12 in (20–30 cm)
Half-hardy annual with a medley of single- and bicolored flowers. Colors include white to pink and red.

THOMPSON & MORGAN

Laurentia axillaris Stars Series
Height: 6 in (15 cm)
Spread: 8–12 in (20–25 cm)
Half-hardy annual, initially forming a dome and later spreading with fragrant flowers in blue, pink or white.

Lobelia erinus – both trailing and compact forms
Edging Lobelia (USA/UK)
Trailing Lobelia (USA/UK)
Height: 4–9 in (10–23 cm)
Spread: 4–9 in (10–23 cm) – some trail
Half-hardy perennial raised as a half-hardy annual, with blue, white or red flowers.

Lobularia maritima
(syn. *Alyssum maritimum*)
Sweet Alyssum (USA/UK)
Height: 3–6 in (7.5–15 cm)
Spread: 8–12 in (20–30 cm)
Hardy annual usually grown as a half-hardy annual, with a wide color range – white, violet-purple and deep purple.

THOMPSON & MORGAN

Lobularia maritima pendula 'Wandering Star'

(syn. *Alyssum maritimum pendula* 'Wandering Star')

Height: 6 in (15 cm)

Trailing nature

Half-hardy annual, with fragrant, cream, purple, pink and rose flowers.

THOMPSON & MORGAN

Nicotiana 'Avalon Lime and Purple Bicolor'

Tobacco Plant (UK)

Height: 8–12 in (20–30 cm)

Spread: 8–12 in (20–30 cm)

Half-hardy annual with a compact nature and large, lime and purple bicolored flowers. Ideal for containers.

THOMPSON & MORGAN

Pansy 'Universal Citrus Mixed'

Garden Pansy (USA/UK)

Pansy (USA/UK)

Height: 6–8 in (15–20 cm)

Spread: 6–10 in (15–25 cm)

Hardy perennial with large, pansy-like flowers in orange, yellow and white.

THOMPSON & MORGAN

Pelargonium 'Regalia'

Height: 9–12 in (23–30 cm)

Spread: 12–15 in (30–38 cm)

Half-hardy annual with flowers in several individual colors, including deep red, pink and white. Unlike many Pelargoniums, it is raised from seeds.

THOMPSON & MORGAN

Petunia milliflora 'Fantasy'

Height: 8–10 in (20–25 cm)

Spread: 10–12 in (25–30 cm)

Half-hardy annual with a compact and miniature habit, bearing masses of loose, trumpet-shaped flowers in a wide range of colors.

THOMPSON & MORGAN

Petunia 'Prism Sunshine'

Height: 10–12 in (25–30 cm)

Spread: 12–15 in (30–38 cm)

Half-hardy annual with large, bright yellow flowers that fade to cream and are often veined in lime-green.

THOMPSON & MORGAN

Petunia 'Wave Series'

Height: 6–8 in (15–20 cm)

Trailing and spreading to 2½ ft (75 cm)

Half-hardy annual with masses of trumpet-shaped flowers; available in single and mixed colors.

THOMPSON & MORGAN

Salvia splendens

Scarlet Salvia (USA/UK)

Height: 12–15 in (30–38 cm)

Spread: 8–10 in (20–25 cm)

Half-hardy perennial invariably grown as a half-hardy annual, with spires of scarlet flowers. Ideal in tubs, troughs and window boxes.

BLUE THEMES

Emotionally, blue creates tranquillity, and for a restful ambience in a garden use this color in hanging baskets and window boxes, where it can be easily seen. Many blues, however, are not clear and cool but more along the color spectrum towards indigo and violet. Pale shades are more towards mauve and create a restful ambience.

Dark blue hanging baskets are more dramatic outdoors than light shades, especially when positioned against a white wall. Light blue hanging-baskets are ideal for vestibules and porches, as well as in conservatories where a non-aggressive display is essential if it is to be a social and restful area.

Sanvitalia procumbens 'Irish Eyes'
Height: 4–6 in (10–15 cm)
Trailing
Half-hardy annual with masses of golden-yellow, double and semi-double flowers, each with an attractive eye. It is ideal for planting in hanging baskets and window boxes, as well as pouches.

Sanvitalia procumbens 'Orange Sprite'
Height: 4–5 in (10–15 cm)
Trailing
Half-hardy annual with a profusion of semi-double orange-colored flowers with dark centers. It is ideal for planting in hanging baskets and window boxes.

Tagetes erecta
Aztec Marigold (USA)
African Marigold (USA/UK)
Height: 2–2½ ft (60–75 cm)
Spread: 12–18 in (30–45 cm)
Half-hardy annual with well-branched stems and lemon-yellow flowers. Other colors range from yellow to orange; some are dwarf.

Tagetes patula
French Marigold (USA/UK)
Height: 12 in (30 cm)
Spread: 10–12 in (25–30 cm)
Half-hardy annual with a bushy nature and yellow or mahogany-red flowers. Single and double-flowered varieties; some have a dwarf nature.

YELLOW THEMES

Yellow is the brightest and most dramatic of all colors and highly visible. It exudes vibrancy and life. However, yellow is a complex color and can include pale cream, demure primrose and fresh lemon, as well as deepening through old gold to orange and bronze. Few patio-brightening features are totally yellow.

Yellow-themed hanging baskets and window boxes are ideal for brightening dull areas where perhaps there is a limited amount of light. Use the strongest yellows and largest flowers for such areas, reserving the more delicately shaped yellow flowers for brighter areas.

Thunbergia alata
Black-eyed Susan (UK)
Black-eyed Susan Vine (USA)
Height: 4–6 ft (1.2–1.8m) – in a pot
Climbing and twining
Half-hardy annual with spectacular, 2 in (5 cm) wide, orange-yellow flowers with dark centers.

Tropaeolum majus (dwarf)
Garden Nasturtium (USA)
Nasturtium (UK)
Height: 15–18 in (38–45 cm)
Climbing and trailing
Half-hardy annual with circular leaves and orange or yellow flowers. Plant in a pot or window box; provide supports.

Verbena erinoides 'Lavender Mist'
Verbena (USA/UK)
Vervain (UK)
Height: 10–12 in (25–30 cm)
Spread: 10–15 in (25–38 cm)
Half-hardy annual with small bunches of pastel-lavender and misty-white flowers.

Verbena x hybrida 'Sandy Mixed'
Verbena (USA/UK)
Vervain (UK)
Height: 8–10 in (20–25 cm)
Spread: 8–12 in (20–30 cm)
Half-hardy, compact annual; flower colors include white, red and carmine.

THOMPSON & MORGAN

Viola x hybrida 'Magnifico'
Viola (USA/UK)
Height: 6–8 in (15–20 cm)
Spread: 6–8 in (15–20 cm)
Half-hardy annual with a compact nature and pure white flowers with violet shading at their edges.

Viola x hybrida 'Penny Orchid Frost'
Viola (USA/UK)
Height: 4–6 in (10–15 cm)
Spread: 6–8 in (15–20 cm)
Half-hardy annual with a compact nature and flowers with orchid-like centers and petals with frost-colored edges.

Viola x wittrockiana 'Flambé Red'
Viola (USA/UK)
Height: 6–9 in (15–23 cm)
Spread: 8–10 in (20–25 cm)
Hardy perennial, raised from seed and with flowers in pastel shades ranging through rose, flame-red and ruby.

Wahlenbergia annularis 'Melton Bicolor'
Rock Bell (UK)
Height: 12–18 in (30–45 cm)
Spread: 15–20 in (38–50 cm)
Half-hardy annual with masses of white, bell-shaped flowers that change to pale blue or pale violet.

RED AND PINK THEMES

Red is a full-blooded and dramatic color, while pink is a desaturated red with a warm and romantic nature; few people do not find pink to be an attractive color. Strongly red designs dominant their surroundings and nearby plants, while pink displays, although at risk of being dominated by stronger colors, nevertheless are often more memorable.

Use strong reds with great care and in limited amounts. Pink, however, can be used in large amounts and still remain attractive. To create a diffused theme, add some white flowers into a pink-themed basket.

Zinnia elegans
Youth and Old Age (USA)
Height: 6–30 in (15–75 cm)
Spread: 6–15 in (15–38 cm)
Half-hardy annual with many varieties and colors, including white, purple, yellow, orange, red and pink. Ideal for window boxes.

OTHER SUMMER-FLOWERING BEDDING PLANTS TO CONSIDER ...

Each year more seed-raised, summer-flowering plants are added to the vast repertoire of plants for growing in containers, and here a few of them.

- *Anagallis linifolia* 'Gentian Blue': blue flowers on plants 6–9 in (15–23 cm) high.
- *Antirrhinum pendula multiflora* 'Chinese Lanterns': superb cascading Antirrhinum with a mixture of seven colors, including pure colors, as well as bicolors. Ideal for hanging baskets and window boxes.
- *Brachycombe iberidifolia* 'Splendour': masses of flowers in blue to purple or white, on plants 9–12 in (23–30 cm) high.
- *Campanula carpatica* 'Bellissimo': plants drenched in chalice-shaped blue or white flowers on plants 6 in (15 cm) high.
- *Gypsophila muralis* 'Gypsy': neat and compact mounds packed with semi- to fully double pink flowers. Ideal for hanging baskets and other containers.
- *Impatiens walleriana* 'Double Carousel Mixed': spectacular, double flowers borne on well-branched plants in a wide range of bright colors.
- *Nemophylla maculata*: light blue flowers with a deep blue spot at the tip of each petal, on plants 3–6 in (7.5–15 cm) high, then trailing.
- *Nemophylla menziesii* 'Pennie Black': purple to black flowers, each about ¾ in (18 mm) wide, on plants 2–4 in (5–10 cm) high and then spreading.
- *Nierembergia* 'Mont Blanc': cup-shaped white flowers on plants 4–6 in (10–15 cm) high.
- *Silene pendula* 'Peach Blossom': masses of double flowers; deep pink when in bud, opening to salmon and maturing to white. Plants grow to about 4–6 in (10–15 cm) high, then cascade.
- *Viola x williamsiana* 'Four Seasons Hybrids': trailing, with sweetly scented small flowers in four individual and different colors – lilac, golden-yellow, purple and violet.

Spring-flowering bedding plants

Spring-flowering bedding plants are invariably hardy biennials raised from seed sown during the previous late spring and early summer and planted into containers in late summer or early autumn. They are inexpensive, and once planted need little attention. Spring-flowering bulbs are other container brighteners in spring, and these are discussed on pages 38–39. Many bulbs are ideal companions for spring-flowering bedding plants (see right).

How do I grow these plants?

HARDY BIENNIALS AND PERENNIALS

Hardy biennials are ideal spring-flowering bedding plants. The term "biennial" means that a plant is sown and raised one year, and produces flowers during the following season. This is a convenient explanation as to how a plant is raised, but not all plants grown as biennials are really biennial.

For example, the popular *Bellis perennis* (Common Daisy) is a hardy perennial invariably raised as a biennial. *Myosotis* (Forget-me-nots) are either biennial or short-lived perennials. The Hollyhock is a hardy perennial usually grown as a biennial, and flowers from mid-summer to early autumn.

THOMPSON & MORGAN

Bellis perennis
Common Daisy (USA/UK)
Height: 2–4 in (5–10 cm)
Spread: 3–4 in (7.5–10 cm)
Bright-faced flowers from early spring to autumn. Many varieties, in white, carmine, pink, salmon or rich cherry.

Erysimum x allionii
(syn. Cheiranthus x allionii)
Siberian Wallflower (UK)
Height: 12–15 in (30–38 cm)
Spread: 10–12 in (25–30 cm)
Masses of fragrant, orange flowers in terminal clusters from mid-spring to early summer. Plant in tubs.

Erysimum alpinum
(syn. E. hieraciifolium)
Alpine Wallflower (UK)
Height: 6 in (15 cm)
Spread: 4–6 in (10–15 cm)
In late spring it bears a mass of fragrant, yellow flowers. There are also varieties with mauve and pale yellow flowers.

Erysimum cheiri
Wallflower (USA/UK)
English Wallflower (USA)
Height: 8–12 in (20–30 cm)
Spread: 6–8 in (15–20 cm)
Fragrant flowers from mid-spring to early summer. Many colors, including orange, blood-red, yellow and rose-pink.

Myosotis sylvatica
Forget-me-not (USA/UK)
Height: 8–12 in (20–30 cm)
Spread: 6 in (15 cm)
Misty-blue flowers in lax sprays during late spring and into early summer. Varieties in several shades of blue.

Primula x polyantha
Polyanthus (USA/UK)
Height: 6–10 in (15–25 cm)
Spread: 6–10 in (15–25 cm)
Superb spring plant in a wide color range, including yellow, cream, white, pink, blue and crimson.

Fragrant spring displays

A wide range of plants can be used to create fragrance and color in spring window boxes. Apart from aromatic dwarf and slow-growing conifers (see page 15), try small bulbs such as:

- *Crocus chrysanthus (sweetly scented, during late winter and spring).*
- *Iris danfordiae (honey-like scent, from mid-winter to early spring).*
- *Iris reticulata (violet bouquet, during late winter and early spring).*
- *Several hardy biennials have deliciously fragrant flowers, including Forget-me-nots and Wallflowers.*

Medleys to consider ...

Mixtures of bulbs and hardy biennials need not be complicated or contain a large number of different plants. Here are several combinations to consider.

- *Try a two-color display with yellow Polyanthus and blue-flowered Muscari armeniacum (Grape Hyacinths).*
- *Plant multi-colored Polyanthus with low-growing trumpet-type Daffodils.*
- *Underplant Tulipa fosteriana or Tulipa greigii with masses of Myosotis (Forget-me-nots). For further color, add double Bellis perennis (Daisies) and Grape Hyacinths.*

ADDING EVERGREEN TRAILERS ...

Small, trailing plants for adding to spring displays have to survive the rigors of winter, and few plants are more suited for this than variegated small-leaved Ivies. They are ideal for planting at the sides of containers. Their range is wide and includes many varieties of *Hedera helix*, the Common Ivy. Garden centers and nurseries offer a wide range of variegated Ivies, and a few to try include:

- 'Elegance': light green, lobed leaves with uneven silver edges.
- 'Glacier': silver-gray, with narrow, white edges.
- 'Gold Child': leaves edged in yellow.
- 'Goldheart' (also known as 'Oro di Bogliasco'): leaves conspicuously splashed gold at their centers.
- 'Pittsburgh': all-green, five-lobed leaves that create a non-attention-seeking yet attractive frill to tubs.
- 'Sagittifolia Variegata': variegated, deeply lobed green leaves with yellow edges.

ADDING EVERGREEN SHRUBS ...

Several variegated evergreen shrubs when small can be added to spring displays in window boxes and troughs to create extra color. They are especially useful should the weather become exceptionally cold or the wind severe, causing damage to hardy biennials and flowers of bulbous plants. Shrubs to consider include:

- *Euonymus fortunei* 'Emerald 'n' Gold': green leaves brightly variegated in gold. They assume bronzy-pink tones in winter. Eventually a moderately large shrub.
- *Hebe* x *andersoniana* 'Variegata': light green leaves that are dominantly edged and splashed in cream.
- *Aucuba japonica* 'Variegata' (Spotted Laurel): shiny green leaves blotched yellow. Eventually forms a large shrub.

ADDING CONIFERS ...

Positioning conifers in window box and trough displays of spring-flowering bedding plants – perhaps with the addition of bulbs – keeps the display attractive for a longer period.

- Several slow-growing and dwarf conifers are featured on pages 34–35, in colors and shapes that introduce contrasts and harmonies. Position short, bushy types at the ends, so that they cloak the edges. Conversely, put taller and upright conifers towards the center to produce a focal point.
- When slow-growing conifers become too large for the container, plant them in tubs on a patio, or in a garden.

VARIEGATED PERIWINKLE

Vinca minor 'Variegata' (Variegated Small-leaved Lesser Periwinkle; also known as *Vinca minor* 'Argenteo-variegata') has small, green leaves that are attractively variegated creamy-white. Additionally, it displays blue flowers from mid-spring to mid-summer – and sometimes later. It is not as invasive as its larger relative, *Vinca major* (Greater Periwinkle).

RAISING BIENNIALS

Biennials are inexpensively raised from seeds sown outdoors during late spring and early summer. In preparation:

- If a piece of ground has not been dug in late autumn or early winter as a site reserved for sowing hardy biennials, in early spring dig a piece of ground, removing all weeds.
- In mid-spring, use a garden fork to break down large lumps and a rake to level the surface. Systematically shuffle sideways over the seed bed to uniformly consolidate the soil. Then, rake the surface level.
- Insert 12 in (30 cm) long sticks 9 in (23 cm) apart on opposite sides of the seed bed.
- Stretch a garden line between two sticks and use a draw-hoe to form a furrow ½ in (12 mm) deep. Alternatively, use a narrow, straight piece of wood for guidance.
- Tip a few seeds into the palm of a hand and slowly dribble them along the row. Ensure they are not touching and are

evenly spaced. If they fall in clusters, it means that extra thinning will be needed later.

- Use the back of a metal rake to carefully push and draw friable soil over the seeds without disturbing them.
- Firm the soil by using the head of the rake.
- Lightly but thoroughly water the soil, taking care not to disturb the surface unnecessarily.
- Place wire-netting or twiggy sticks over the furrows to prevent birds disturbing the seeds.
- When the seedlings are large enough to handle, either thin them out or transfer to a nursery bed. For small plants such as Daisies, thin seedlings to about 4 in (10 cm) apart; for larger biennials such as Wallflowers thin to 6 in (15 cm).
- Transfer the plants to containers in early autumn, especially if the container is also to hold bulbs, which are planted about the same time.

Hardy border perennials

How do I grow these plants?

Border plants are perennial, and last from one season to another, until they become too large for the container and need to be removed, divided and put into another container or a garden border. Some hardy border perennials have a herbaceous nature – the leaves die down in autumn or early winter and fresh ones appear in spring or early summer. Other border plants will retain their foliage throughout all or most of the year.

LOOKING AFTER BORDER PERENNIALS

These plants usually need little attention, except to remove damaged leaves and dead flowers throughout the season, and to pull or cut off stems and leaves from those plants that die down each year. However, some of these plants – especially Hostas – can be badly damaged by slugs and snails, especially when positioned in slight shade and on damp patios. Pellets and baits help to prevent damage, as well as placing containers – if their size is right – on inverted pots or in wire frames.

BORDER PERENNIALS IN CONTAINERS

The main difficulty when growing border perennials in containers is to keep the soil moist throughout summer, as well as relatively dry in winter. Soil rich in peat helps to retain moisture, but if it should become dry it is far more difficult to remoisten. Regularly watering the soil is the main task during hot summers.

In winter, water-saturated soil is likely to freeze and cause damage to roots. Plants that have soft, tuberous roots are most at risk. Covering the surface of the soil with straw helps to keep the soil dry, and thereby prevents it from freezing.

Aegopodium podagraria **'Variegatum'**
Variegated Gout Weed (USA)
Variegated Ground Elder (USA/UK)
Height: 6–10 in (15–25 cm)
Spread: Forms a clump
Light to mid-green leaves edged in white, even when grown in light shade.

Agapanthus **'Lilliput'**
African Lily (USA/UK)
Height: 18 in (45 cm)
Spread: 10–12 in (25–30 cm)
Narrow, green leaves and upright stems bearing umbrella-like heads of blue flowers during mid- and late summer.

Agave americana **'Variegata'**
Variegated Century Plant (USA/UK)
Height: 2½–3 ft (75–90 cm)
Spread: 2–2½ ft (60–75 cm)
Tender succulent with thick, sword-like, gray-green leaves with yellow edges. Needs frost-free winter conditions.

Ajuga reptans
Bugle (USA/UK)
Height: 4–12 in (10–30 cm)
Spread: 12–18 in (30–45 cm)
Spreading herbaceous perennial with whorls of blue flowers in early and mid-summer. Several colored-leaf forms.

Alchemilla mollis
Lady's Mantle (USA/UK)
Height: 12–18 in (30–45 cm)
Spread: 15–20 in (38–50 cm)
Herbaceous perennial that has light green, lobed leaves, and produces masses of sulphur-yellow flowers from early to late summer.

SELECTING SUITABLE PLANTS

Some border perennials are not suited to life in a container, especially when tall and needing support. Here are a few indicators that will help you to choose the right plants:

- Select relatively low-growing plants, especially if your patio is exposed to strong and gusting wind.
- Choose plants that have both interesting flowers and attractive leaves, especially if the flowering period is short. Hostas have the dual role, and there are many from which to choose (see page 26).
- If the leaves remain throughout winter, select plants which have a domed outline and create little resistance to wind. Such plants are also less likely to be damaged by heavy snowfalls, although it is always wise to gently remove snow at the first opportunity.
- Select winter-brightening plants as well as those that reveal their qualities during summer. Winter flowers are always cherished. Frost on the leaves of plants can provide a further winter attraction.

CONTAINER COMPANIONS

Agapanthus in Versailles planters – see below right for plants.

Stachys byzantina in low Ali Baba type pots – see page 29 for plants.

Anthemis punctata subsp. **cupaniana**
Golden Marguerite (USA/UK)
Height: 6–10 in (15–25 cm)
Spread: 12–15 in (30–38 cm)
Short-lived herbaceous perennial with bright-faced, daisy-like, yellow-centered white flowers from early to late summer.

Aquilegia McKana Hybrids
Granny's Bonnet (UK)
European Columbine (USA)
Height: 2–2½ ft (60–75 cm)
Spread: 12–15 in (30–38 cm)
Herbaceous perennial with cream, yellow, pink, red, crimson or blue flowers during late spring and early summer.

Astilbe x arendsii
Height: 1½–2 ft (45–60 cm)
Spread: 15–20 in (38–50 cm)
Hardy herbaceous perennial with feather-like flower plumes in various colors from early to late summer.

Bergenia cordifolia
Elephant's Ears (UK)
Height: 10–12 in (23–30 cm)
Spread: 12–15 in (30–38 cm)
Hardy border plant with evergreen, rounded leaves and clusters of bell-shaped flowers in early and mid-spring.

Crocosmia x crocosmiiflora
Montbretia (USA/UK)
Height: 1½–2 ft (45–60 cm)
Spread: Clump-forming
Slightly tender cormous plant for a tub, with funnel-shaped flowers from mid- to late summer, in colors ranging from yellow to deep red.

Dicentra spectabilis
Bleeding Heart (USA/UK)
Height: 18–30 in (45–75 cm)
Spread: 18–20 in (45–50 cm)
Hardy herbaceous perennial with distinctive, heart-shaped, rose-red and white flowers during early summer.

OTHER AGAPANTHUS ...

Agapanthus seldom fail to attract attention, and they are ideal plants for a tub or other large container. Their range is wide, and includes:

- *Agapanthus praecox*: a half-hardy perennial, which produces magnificent umbrella-like heads of bright to pale blue flowers. There is also a white-flowered form.
- *Agapanthus* 'Headbourne Hybrids': hardier than species types, with distinctive flower heads in colors from violet-blue to pale blue.
- *Agapanthus campanulatus* 'Isis': this is a superb plant with a free-flowering habit, producing many heads of deep blue flowers.

Doronicum plantagineum

Leopard's Bane (USA/UK)
Height: 1½–2½ ft (45–75 cm)
Spread: 15 in (38 cm)
Hardy herbaceous perennial with large, daisy-like, bright yellow flowers during late spring and early summer.

Epimedium perralderianum

Barrenwort (UK)
Bishop's Hat (UK)
Height: 8–12 in (20–30 cm)
Spread: 12–18 in (30–45 cm)
Hardy, evergreen perennial with leaves at first bright green, becoming coppery-bronze in autumn. Yellow flowers.

HOSTAS FOR CONTAINERS

The range of Hostas has increased dramatically in recent years and there are many superb plants, including:

- *Hosta sieboldiana*: glossy-green leaves and dull white flowers.
- 'Blue Moon': small, deep blue leaves and grayish-mauve flowers.
- 'Golden Prayers': golden-yellow leaves and mauve flowers.
- 'Shade Fanfare': green leaves with broad, cream edges. The green becomes yellow when the plant is positioned in full sunlight.
- 'Wide Brim': oval, blue-green leaves irregularly edged in cream to golden-yellow. Lavender-colored flowers.

Geranium endressii

Crane's-bill (USA/UK)
Height: 12–18 in (30–45 cm)
Spread: 15–18 in (38–45 cm)
Hardy herbaceous perennial with pale pink flowers from early summer to autumn. Many superb varieties.

Hakonechloa macra 'Aureola'

Height: 10–12 in (25–30 cm)
Spread: 2½–3 ft (75–90 cm)
Hardy, cascading perennial grass with narrow, bright yellow leaves striped green. There are other superb forms.

Helleborus niger

Christmas Rose (USA/UK)
Height: 12–18 in (30–45 cm)
Spread: 15–18 in (38–45 cm)
Hardy perennial with evergreen leaves. From mid-winter to early spring it bears white, saucer-shaped flowers.

DORONICUMS TO CONSIDER ...

Several superb varieties of this early-summer brightener are ideal for containers. Their strongly yellow flowers soon capture attention, but ensure that they do not dominate plants with demure flowers. Select low-growing types. Varieties to try include:

- 'Harpur Crewe': distinctive, with golden-yellow flowers up to 3 in (7.5 cm) wide.
- 'Miss Mason': grows to about 18 in (45 cm) high, with bright yellow flowers up to 2½ in (6 cm) wide.
- 'Spring Beauty': grows to about 15 in (38 cm) high with double, deep-yellow flowers.

Helleborus orientalis

Lenten Rose (UK)
Height: 18–24 in (45–60 cm)
Spread: 18 in (45 cm)
Hardy perennial with evergreen leaves. During late winter and early spring it has cream flowers flecked with crimson.

Hemerocallis thunbergii

Day Lily (USA/UK)
Height: 2½–3 ft (75–90 cm)
Spread: 2 ft (60 cm)
Hardy herbaceous perennial with large, trumpet-shaped, sulphur-apricot flowers during early and mid-summer.

Heuchera sanguinea
Coral Flower (UK)
Coral Bells (USA)
Height: 12–15 in (30–38 cm)
Spread: 12–15 in (30–38 cm)
Hardy evergreen herbaceous perennial with small, bright red flowers. 'Alba,' with yellow flowers, is shown above.

Hosta fortunei var. albopicta
Plantain Lily (USA/UK)
Height: 15–18 in (38–45 cm)
Spread: 18 in (45 cm)
Hardy herbaceous perennial with pale green leaves variegated buff-yellow. There are many other superb varieties.

Houttuynia cordata 'Chameleon'
Height: 6–10 in (15–25 cm)
Spread: Spreading and branching
Hardy herbaceous perennial with leaves that have a patchwork of yellow, green, bronze and red. Small, white flowers.

Lamium maculatum
Dead Nettle (UK)
White Dead Nettle (USA)
Height: 6–9 in (15–23 cm)
Spread: Spreading
Hardy herbaceous perennial with mid-green leaves with a central silver stripe. Pink-purple flowers in late spring.

Liatris spicata
Blazing Star (USA/UK)
Gayfeather (USA/UK)
Height: 2 ft (60 cm)
Spread: 12–18 in (30–45 cm)
Hardy, tuberous-rooted herbaceous perennial with spires of pinkish-purple flowers in late summer and into autumn.

Limonium latifolium
Sea Lavender (USA/UK)
Statice (USA)
Height: 1½–2 ft (45–60 cm)
Spread: 1½ ft (45 cm)
Hardy perennial with leathery, dark green leaves. From mid- to late summer it bears clouds of lavender-blue flowers.

OTHER HEMEROCALLIS TO CONSIDER ...

Many of the colorful *Hemerocallis* hybrids are well worth planting in tubs. These include:
- 'Black Magic': ruby purple with a distinctive yellow throat.
- 'Buzz Bomb': rich velvety-red.
- 'Cartwheels': large, bright yellow flowers that open to create large and nearly flat heads.
- 'Little Wine Cup': dwarf plant, with burgundy flowers; golden throats.
- 'Pink Damask': superb plant, with warm pink flowers that reveal a yellow throat.
- 'Stella D'Oro': dwarf plant, with canary-yellow, bell-shaped flowers with an orange throat.

GERANIUM OR PELARGONIUM?

Geraniums and Pelargoniums are frequently confused with each other, especially as Pelargoniums are popularly known as Geraniums.
- Geraniums are herbaceous perennials grown mainly in gardens but also in tubs and other large containers on patios and terraces. They are hardy and can be left outdoors all year.
- Pelargoniums are warmth-loving shrubs – mainly from southern Africa – that in temperate climates are raised as tender plants for growing in pots, tubs and other containers. They create magnificent displays outdoors in summer, but are soon killed by low temperatures.

OTHER LAMIUMS TO CONSIDER ...

These are durable perennials and ideal for creating color in tubs. They are often erroneously considered not to be sufficiently attractive for planting in containers, but they thrive in sun or shade. Here are a few to try:
- 'Album': mid-green leaves with a central silver stripe; white flowers.
- 'Aureum': slow-growing, with attractive golden foliage. It is best positioned in full sun in order to encourage the development of bright-colored leaves.
- 'Roseum': mid-green leaves with a central silver stripe; the flowers are shell-pink.

Lysimachia nummularia

Creeping Jenny (USA/UK)

Moneywort (USA/UK)

Height: 2–3 in (5–7.5 cm)

Spread: Trailing to about 1½ ft (45 cm)

Hardy evergreen plant with prostrate stems with mid-green leaves and yellow flowers during early and mid-summer.

Lysimachia nummularia 'Aurea'

Yellow-leaved Moneywort (USA/UK)

Height: 2–3 in (5–7.5 cm)

Spread: Trailing to about 1½ ft (45 cm)

Hardy evergreen plant with prostrate stems, beautiful yellow leaves and yellow flowers in early and mid-summer.

Melissa officinalis 'Aurea'

Golden Balm (USA/UK)

Height: 2½ ft (75 cm)

Spread: 12–18 in (30–45 cm)

Hardy herbaceous perennial (it is a form of the well-known Balm) that has golden-green leaves.

GROWING GRASSES IN CONTAINERS

Many grasses are ideal for growing in containers and positioning on patios, terraces and around houses. Some have a cascading habit that creates an attractive outline and clothes the upper edges of the container. Regular watering is essential to ensure that the relatively small amount of compost does not become dry.

In addition to the superb grass *Hakonechloa macra* 'Aureola' there are other varieties to consider, including 'Alboaurea' with leaves striped off-white and gold; in autumn they assume rich pink and red shades.

There are several grasses that can be used to create attractive features in containers. These include:

- *Acorus gramineus* 'Ogon': initially it has an upright habit, then is arching and more relaxed, with narrow, tapering green leaves with golden variegated bands along their lengths. Other variegated forms include 'Hakuro-nishiki,' 'Variegatus' with leaves striped cream and yellow, and 'Yodo-no-yuki' with leaves variegated pale green.
- *Carex oshimensis* 'Evergold': it has an attractive arching nature, with leaves variegated green and yellow.
- *Festuca glauca*: this grass has a tufted habit, and there are varieties with colored leaves – including blue, blue-green and silvery-blue – which are extremely popular.

Monarda didyma

Bee Balm (USA/UK)

Oswego Tea (USA/UK)

Height: 2–3 ft (60–90 cm)

Spread: 15–18 in (38–45 cm)

Hardy herbaceous perennial with dense heads of scarlet flowers throughout summer. There are several varieties.

Osteospermum ecklonis var. prostratum

African Daisy (UK)

Height: 6–9 in (15–23 cm)

Spread: 12–15 in (30–38 cm)

Bushy perennial with masses of daisy-like, white flowers with mustard-yellow centers in mid- and late summer.

Pachysandra terminalis 'Variegata'

Variegated Japanese Spurge (USA)

Height: 8–10 in (20–25 cm)

Spread: 12–15 in (30–38 cm)

Hardy, sub-shrubby plant with green leaves edged in white. It is ideal for smothering compost in a large tub.

Phormium tenax

New Zealand Flax (USA/UK)

New Zealand Hemp (USA/UK)

Height: 5–8 ft (1.5–2.4 m)

Spread: 4–5 ft (1.2–1.5 m)

Perennial, hardy in all but the coldest positions, with mid- to deep-green leaves (several colored forms).

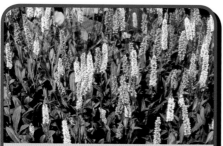

Polygonum affine 'Dimity'
Knotweed (USA/UK)
Height: 6–8 in (15–20 cm)
Spread: 12 in (30 cm)
Hardy herbaceous perennial with spoon-shaped green leaves and deep-pink flowers throughout summer and into autumn.

Pulmonaria officinalis
Blue Lungwort (USA)
Jerusalem Sage (USA/UK)
Height: 12 in (30 cm)
Spread: 12 in (30 cm)
Hardy herbaceous perennial with white-spotted green leaves. Purple-blue flowers in late spring and early summer.

OTHER STACHYS TO TRY ...

Although *Stachys byzantina* is not fully hardy in all areas, where it is sheltered from cold and excessive wet weather it creates interest throughout the year. There are several attractive forms to consider growing, including:
- 'Cotton Boll' (also known as 'Sheila Macqueen'): it has large, felted, gray-green leaves and silvery flowers.
- 'Primrose Heron': this is a superb plant for year-round interest. During the summer, the leaves create a glorious golden carpet.
- 'Silver Carpet': this is an excellent plant with silky, silver leaves. It does not develop any flowers.

Sedum 'Autumn Joy'
Ice Plant (USA/UK)
Height: 18–24 in (45–60 cm)
Spread: 18–20 in (45–50 cm)
Hardy herbaceous perennial with fleshy leaves and heads of salmon-pink flowers that change to orange-brown in autumn.

Sempervivum tectorum
Common Houseleek (USA/UK)
Hens and Chicks (USA)
Height: 2–3 in (5–7.5 cm)
Spread: 6–12 in (15–30 cm)
Hardy, rosette-forming evergreen succulent with mid-green leaves with maroon tips. Rose-purple flowers are produced in mid-summer.

Stachys byzantina
Lamb's Tongue (UK)
Lamb's Ears (USA/UK)
Height: 12–18 in (30–45 cm)
Spread: 12–15 in (30–38 cm)
Half-hardy perennial with foliage that persists throughout the year. Leaves have a silvery and woolly appearance.

Tiarella cordifolia
Foam Flower (USA/UK)
Height: 9–12 in (23–30 cm)
Spread: 9–12 in (23–30 cm)
Hardy, low-growing, evergreen perennial with maple-like mid-green leaves and spires of creamy-white flowers.

Tolmiea menziesii
Piggyback Plant (USA/UK)
Youth-on-Age (USA/UK)
Height: 6–8 in (15–20 cm)
Spread: 12–15 in (30–38 cm)
Hardy evergreen with maple-like green leaves and spires of flowers on stems up to 2 ft (60 cm) high in early summer.

OTHER PHORMIUMS TO CONSIDER ...

Many Phormiums have colorful leaves that create spectacular features when in large containers on a patio or terrace. In areas where the temperature falls radically in winter, protect plants from severe frost. Incidentally, the all-green type is hardier than the variegated forms. Here are two forms of *Phormium tenax* to consider:
- 'Purpureum': this has superb, bronze-purple leaves.
- 'Variegatum': the leaves are striped green and yellow.
Additionally, there are some excellent forms of *Phormium cookianum* (also known as *Phormium colensoi*).

Flowering shrubs

Shrubs have a perennial, woody nature, and although some are quite short-lived most will thrive in tubs until they outgrow their containers and have to be planted out in a garden. Select tubs or large pots for shrubs, using rustic tubs for those with an informal appearance. Large pots are more clinical in appearance and are ideal for shrubs with a formal and well-defined outline. Good drainage is essential, and you should always use soil-based compost.

POSITIONING FLOWERING SHRUBS

Unlike those shrubs that have attractive evergreen foliage, flowering types do not create interest throughout the year. Therefore, it is best not to use them as year-round focal points. Instead, position them in clusters with other shrubs, but without intruding on their outlines. Most flowering shrubs prefer a sunny position, but Camellias require a situation that is out of direct and early-morning sunlight. Watering is essential throughout the summer, and especially when shrubs are flowering. Make sure, however, that the soil does not become waterlogged by winter rains.

ROSES IN TUBS AND POTS

Planting Roses in tubs and pots is an exciting way to grow them on patios and terraces – or in small gardens. They are deciduous shrubs – choose either Miniature or Patio Roses.

Miniature Roses are best planted in large pots and where a soil depth of at least 9 in (23 cm) is possible. Patio Roses are slightly larger and are better in tubs, where a soil depth of 12 in (30 cm) is possible. Buy soil specifically formulated for container-grown shrubs.

Suitable Miniature Roses:
• 'Angela Rippon': this has clusters of small, double, rosy salmon-pink, lightly scented flowers.
• 'Darling Flame': it has small, double, orange-red, lightly scented flowers.
• 'Rise 'n' Shine' (also known as 'Golden Sunblaze'): this rose produces clusters of small, double, golden-yellow flowers.
• 'Starina': small, double, orange-red flowers are borne on bushy plants.

Suitable Patio Roses:
• 'Anna Ford': clusters of vivid orange-red flowers with a yellow base.
• 'Conservation': bushy plants, with lightly scented, apricot-pink flowers.
• 'Gentle Touch': clusters of small, double pale-pink flowers.
• 'Peek-a-boo': clusters of small, double, apricot to pink flowers.
• 'Sweet Magic': clusters of small, double, moderately fragrant, orange flowers with golden tints.

Azaleas (Japanese) – evergreen types
Height: 1½–2 ft (45–60 cm)
Spread: 2–2½ ft (60–75 cm)
Small-leaved, bushy plants with masses of funnel-shaped flowers in spring. Colors include scarlet, pink and white. Use a slightly acid, loam-based compost.

Camellia x williamsii
Camellia (USA/UK)
Height: 5–6 ft (1.5–1.8 m)
Spread: 4–5 ft (1.2–1.5 m)
Evergreen, in colors from white and pale-pink to rose-purple. Flowering mainly in late winter and spring.

Choisya ternata
Mexican Orange Flower (USA/UK)
Height: 5–6 ft (1.5–1.8 m)
Spread: 5–7 ft (1.5–2.1m)
Slightly tender evergreen shrub with scented, orange-blossom-like flowers mainly during mid- and late summer.

INEXPENSIVE ROSEMARY

Planting a large tub with three Rosemary plants can be expensive. Therefore, economize and take cuttings.
Step by step to success:
• In mid-summer, take 3–4 in (7.5–10 cm) long cuttings and insert them in pots containing equal parts of moist peat and coarse sand.
• Place them outdoors in a cold frame or unheated greenhouse.
• When rooted, transfer them to 3 in (7.5 cm) wide pots and overwinter them in a cold frame.
• Plant into a tub in spring. For a display that quickly fills a tub, plant five or seven cuttings in it.

Doronicum hirsutum (syn. *Lotus hirsutus*)

Height: 12–15 in (30–38 cm) in a container

Spread: 15–18 in (38–45 cm) in a container

Hardy, semi-herbaceous, woody-based shrub with heads of white, pink-flushed flowers in late summer and autumn.

Genista pilosa 'Vancouver Gold'

Broom (USA/UK)

Height: 6–12 in (15–30 cm)

Spread: 3–4 ft (90 cm–1.2 m)

Compact, evergreen shrub with masses of deep golden-yellow flowers during late spring and early summer.

Hebe 'Margret'

Shrubby Veronica (UK)

Height: 12–15 in (30–38 cm)

Spread: 1½–2 ft (45–60 cm)

Dwarf, compact, evergreen shrub that produces sky-blue flowers in late spring and early summer. It often also flowers in late summer.

Hydrangea macrophylla

Common Hydrangea (UK)

French Hydrangea (USA)

Height: 3–4 ft (60 cm–1.2 m) in a tub

Spread: 4–5 ft (1.2–1.5 m) in a tub

Hardy deciduous shrub: use Hortensia types, with flower heads 5–8 in (13–20 cm) wide in mid-summer to early autumn.

Hypericum olympicum

Height: 8–12 in (20–30 cm)

Spread: 12–15 in (30–38 cm)

Hardy, low-growing evergreen shrub with golden-yellow flowers, about 1½ in (36 mm) wide, in mid-summer.

Magnolia stellata

Star Magnolia (USA/UK)

Height: 5–6 ft (1.5–1.8 m) in a tub

Spread: 5–6 ft (1.5–1.8 m) in a tub

Hardy, slow-growing deciduous shrub with fragrant, white, large, star-like flowers during early and mid-spring.

Rosmarinus officinalis

Rosemary (USA/UK)

Height: 2–2½ ft (60–75 cm) in a tub

Spread: 2–2½ ft (60–75 cm) in a tub

Hardy, evergreen shrub with aromatic leaves and mauve flowers during spring, and intermittently later.

OTHER FLOWERING SHRUBS TO CONSIDER ...

- *Erica carnea*: a low-growing but bushy, evergreen shrub with flowers in many colors from late autumn to late spring.
- *Fuchsia magellanica*: a slightly tender shrub with crimson and purple, pendent flowers from mid-summer to autumn.
- *Hypericum* x *moserianum*: an evergreen shrub with a spreading nature and rich-yellow flowers from mid-summer to autumn. There is also the form 'Tricolor' which has attractively variegated leaves.
- *Lavandula angustifolia* 'Hidcote': a hardy, evergreen shrub with narrow, silvery-gray leaves and deep purple-blue flowers from mid- to late summer.
- *Mahonia* 'Charity': eventually a tall, evergreen shrub with arching spires of fragrant, deep yellow flowers from late autumn to late winter. Position it in a wind-sheltered corner, in full sun or dappled light.
- *Prunus incisa* 'Kojo Nomal': a small, flowering, ornamental cherry with red-centered pink flowers in spring.
- *Rhododendron yakushimanum*: a small, evergreen shrub with dark green leaves that produces masses of pink flowers, which later fade to white, during late spring and early summer.

Foliage shrubs

How do I grow foliage shrubs?

Tubs and large pots are essential when growing shrubs in containers. Some of these shrubs are evergreen and create attractive features throughout the year, while a few are deciduous. Some shrubs, as well as being deciduous and creating a fresh array of foliage each year, have leaves that assume rich colors in autumn before falling. Deciduous foliage shrubs tend to be slightly hardier than evergreen types, and therefore can be positioned in cooler places.

FOLIAGE SHRUBS FOR MEDITERRANEAN-STYLE GARDENS

Several of the foliage shrubs described on these pages will recall memories of vacations in warm climates, such as in Mediterranean countries. Yuccas and Cordylines create the impression of clinical warmth, while *Trachycarpus fortunei* (Chinese Windmill Palm) is a more dominant and distinctive

plant. *Fatsia japonica* (False Castor Oil Plant) is another scene-setting plant for warm areas, and with the bonus of attractive foliage and distinctive white flowers in the autumn. Do not confuse this plant with *Ricinus communis* (Castor Oil Plant), which is best avoided.

COLORFUL SAGES ...

Several forms of the popular culinary Sage *Salvia officinalis* are ideal in containers. It is a short-lived, slightly tender shrubby plant that after a few years needs replacement when it becomes straggly. There are three superb forms with colored leaves; they grow about 1½–2 ft (45–60 cm) high and with a 15–18 in (38–45 cm) spread – sometimes more:

- 'Icterina': superb green-and-gold leaves. It creates a dominant display.
- 'Purpurescens': stems and leaves suffused purple when young.
- 'Tricolor': gray-green leaves splashed creamy-white and suffused with pink and purple.

Acer palmatum 'Dissectum Atropurpureum'
Height: 3–4 ft (90 cm–1.2 m) in a tub
Spread: 4–5 ft (1.2–1.5 m) in a tub
Hardy deciduous shrub with finely dissected bronze-red leaves. A closely related form has all-green leaves.

Aucuba japonica 'Variegata'
Gold Dust Plant (USA)
Spotted Laurel (USA)
Height: 3½–4½ ft (1–1.3 m) in a tub
Spread: 3–4 ft (90 cm–1.2 m) in a tub
Hardy, bushy, evergreen shrub with a dome-like outline and dark green leaves peppered and splashed with yellow.

Choisya ternata 'Sundance'
Yellow-leaved Mexican Orange Blossom (USA/UK)
Height: 2½–3½ ft (75 cm–1 m) in a tub
Spread: 2½–3 ft (75–90 cm) in a tub
Slightly tender evergreen shrub with golden-yellow leaves all year round.

Elaeagnus pungens 'Maculata'
Variegated Thorny Elaeagnus (USA)
Height: 5–6 ft (1.5–1.8 m) in a tub
Spread: 5–6 ft (1.5–1.8 m) in a tub
Hardy, evergreen shrub with leathery, glossy-green leaves splashed with gold. Superb for winter color.

Euonymus fortunei 'Emerald 'n' Gold'
Height: 12–18 in (30–45 cm)
Spread: 18–24 in (45–60 cm)
Hardy evergreen shrub, densely covered with golden leaves that turn bronzy-pink in winter. Many other varieties.

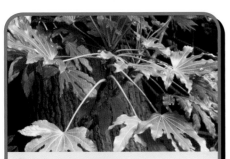

Fatsia japonica
False Castor Oil Plant (UK)

Glossy-leaved Paper Plant (USA)

Height: 5–7 ft (1.5–2.1 m)

Spread: 5–6 ft (1.5–1.8 m)

Slightly tender evergreen shrub with large, glossy, hand-like green leaves, and white flowers in autumn.

Hebe x andersonii 'Variegata'
Shrubby Veronica (USA/UK)

Height: 2½–3 ft (75–90 cm)

Spread: 2–3 ft (60–90 cm)

Slightly tender evergreen shrub with cream and green leaves. Lavender flowers from mid-summer to autumn.

Hebe x franciscana
Shrubby Veronica (USA/UK)

Height: 12–18 in (30–45 cm)

Spread: 12–18 in (30–45 cm)

Slightly tender evergreen shrub with a dome-shaped outline and glossy-green leaves edged cream. Mauve-blue flowers.

Lonicera nitida 'Baggeson's Gold'
Yellow-leaved Chinese Honeysuckle (USA/UK)

Height: 3–5 ft (90 cm–1.5 m) in a tub

Spread: 2½–3 ft (75–90 cm) in a tub

Hardy evergreen shrub with small, golden leaves. It can be clipped.

Trachycarpus fortunei
Chinese Windmill Palm (USA/UK)

Chusan Palm (UK)

Height: 6–7 ft (1.8–2.1 m) in a tub

Spread: 5–6 ft (1.5–1.8 m) in a tub

Slightly tender, evergreen, slow-growing palm with large fans of glossy, mid-green leaves borne on long stalks.

Yucca filamentosa 'Variegata'
Variegated Adam's Needle (USA/UK)

Height: 2–2½ ft (60–75 cm)

Spread: 3–4 ft (90 cm–1.2 m)

Slightly tender evergreen shrub with rosettes of deep green leaves handsomely edged in whitish-yellow.

OTHER FOLIAGE SHRUBS TO CONSIDER ...

- *Berberis thunbergii* 'Aurea': superb hardy deciduous shrub with masses of bright, soft yellow leaves. There are several other colorfully leaved varieties, including 'Atropurpurea' (rich purple-red) and 'Atropurpurea 'Nana' (a dwarf form with rich purple-red leaves).
- *Calluna vulgaris*: hardy evergreen shrub with a low-growing habit. There are many attractively foliaged varieties, including 'Beoley Gold' (golden-yellow), 'Blazeaway' (foliage changes from gold through orange to red), 'Gold Haze' (bright gold) and 'Golden Carpet' (golden foliage flecked with orange and red during winter).
- *Cordyline australis* 'Purpurea': often known as a Cabbage Tree, it is slow-growing and has narrow, purple leaves. There are varieties in other colors.
- *Eucalyptus gunnii*: known as the Cider Gum and relatively hardy in temperate regions, this evergreen tree has a shrubby habit. It needs to be radically pruned in mid- to late spring to encourage the development of its distinctive juvenile foliage, which is round and blue-green. It needs a wind-sheltered position in full sun.
- *Hebe pinquifolia* 'Pagei': a low, evergreen shrub with small, gray leaves. During early summer, it has the bonus of bearing small, white flowers.
- *Ligustrum ovalifolium* 'Aureum': this is the Golden-leaved Privet, with rich golden-yellow leaves with green centers that certainly bring brightness to a patio.
- *Nandina domestica*: this is commonly known as the Chinese Sacred Bamboo, although it is not a bamboo. It has a slightly tender nature but grows well in containers on a sheltered patio. The leaf color changes from red, when the plant is young, to mid-green.
- *Sambucus racemosa* 'Sutherland Gold': eventually a large, deciduous shrub, but when young is ideal in a large tub. It has finely cut, golden-yellow leaves.

Dwarf and slow-growing conifers

Miniature and slow-growing conifers are well suited for growing in tubs and pots, as well as old stone sinks and firm-based troughs. They can also be planted in window boxes as part of a winter display. Well-drained, loam-based soil is essential, as well as good drainage. Once established, conifers are easy to grow and need little attention, although eventually most of them become too large for the container and are planted in the garden.

POSITIONING CONIFERS IN CONTAINERS

One of the main dangers to conifers when grown in containers, especially if planted in relatively small pots as compared with tubs, is that tall types are at risk from being blown over by gusting winds. Therefore, position them in the shelter of a wall. An additional safeguard is to plant wind-susceptible conifers in large or heavy-based containers, such as those formed of reconstituted stone. Also, use loam-based soil rather than a peat-based type. Other dangers are the soil becoming dry during summer, and excessively wet in winter when there is little chance of it drying.

Chamaecyparis lawsoniana 'Ellwoodii'
Slow-growing and ideal when small for planting in a container. It has short, feathery sprays of gray-green foliage that, in winter, assume shades of steel-blue. The form 'Ellwood's Golden Pillar' has golden-yellow foliage.

Chamaecyparis pisifera 'Boulevard'
Slow-growing, with a dense, narrowly conical outline packed with steel-blue foliage. The foliage is feathery and it is usually at its brightest when positioned in light shade. Plant it in a tub.

Chamaecyparis pisifera 'Filifera Aurea'
Slow-growing and very distinctive conifer, with a conical outline and spreading branches bearing drooping branchlets of thread-like, golden-yellow foliage. Eventually it forms a mop-headed plant. Plant it in a tub.

Juniperus chinensis 'Pyramidalis'
Slow-growing conifer with a conical outline and dense nature with dull, dark green leaves. The younger leaves have a bluish tinge and this creates an attractive feature when sunlight glances off them. Plant it in a tub.

Juniperus communis 'Depressa Aurea'
Slow-growing, with a spreading nature and packed with beautiful foliage, golden-yellow when young. With its spreading and, eventually, slightly mop-headed outline, it is best planted in a tub.

Juniperus communis 'Hibernica'
Slow-growing, with a columnar outline but, eventually, more narrowly oval. It is packed with needle-like, silver-backed leaves. When small it is ideal for window boxes, then large tubs and, eventually, the garden.

Juniperus scopularium 'Skyrocket'

Also known as *Juniperus virginiana* 'Skyrocket,' it has a slow-growing, narrow habit and upright branches bearing silvery, blue-gray foliage. It has a distinctive outline and is best planted in a tub.

Juniperus squamata 'Blue Star'

Slow-growing, low conifer densely packed with silvery-blue foliage. It has a squat nature, but with shoots that attractively break the regularity of its outline. Plant it in a tub.

Juniperus squamata 'Meyeri'

A vigorous, semi-erect conifer which when young and before it becomes too large is ideal for growing in a tub. It is densely packed with glaucous-blue leaves and is ideal for creating a dominant blue feature on a patio.

Pinus sylvestris 'Beuvronensis'

Distinctive, miniature Scots Pine that creates a low, broad, cone-like outline of gray-green foliage. It is especially attractive in spring when new growth appears and is ideal for planting in a tub.

Taxus baccata 'Standishii'

Slow-growing, densely columnar conifer packed with golden-yellow leaves. It is ideal for creating a shape contrast on a patio and although at first it can be planted in a large pot, eventually it needs a tub to provide stability.

Thuja orientalis 'Aurea Nana'

Also known as *Platycladus orientalis* 'Aurea Nana,' it is slow-growing with a neat, rounded habit. Ideal for planting first in a large pot, later transferring it to a tub. It reveals beautiful light yellow-green foliage and is especially attractive when positioned in full sun.

Thuja plicata 'Stoneham Gold'

Slow-growing, with a conical outline and bright golden foliage with coppery-bronze tips. Initially, plant it in a large pot, but later transfer to a tub.

OTHER CONIFERS TO CONSIDER ...

- *Abies balsamea* 'Hudsonia': dense and compact, with closely arranged short leaves that emit the fragrance of balsam.
- *Abies lasiocarpa* var. *arizonica* 'Compacta': slow-growing with a dense, conical outline. Attractive blue-gray foliage.
- *Chamaecyparis lawsoniana* 'Aurea Densa': slow-growing and compact with densely packed, golden-yellow foliage in short, flattened sprays.
- *Chamaecyparis lawsoniana* 'Minima Aurea': dwarf and slow-growing, with a conical outline and sprays of soft, golden-yellow foliage.
- *Juniperus communis* 'Compressa': slow-growing, with a columnar habit and narrow, prickly, silver-backed leaves. It is ideal for planting in window boxes, as well as in pots and troughs.
- *Juniperus horizontalis* 'Wiltonii': slow-growing, with long branches packed with glaucous-blue foliage. Plant it in a tub.
- *Juniperus* x *pfitzeriana* 'Old Gold': also known as *Juniperus* x *media* 'Old Gold,' it has a compact habit and bronze-gold foliage.
- *Thuja occidentalis* 'Rheingold': slow-growing, with a conical outline and rich, old-gold foliage with a hint of amber.

Bamboos

Are bamboos suitable for containers?

Many bamboos grow remarkably well in containers that can be positioned on a patio, terrace or around a house. They create color and interest throughout the year. Some have variegated leaves, while others are totally green. Some have colored canes. Several tall bamboos with small leaves produce an attractive rustling sound when blown by even the slightest breeze, and this introduces a relaxing and soothing quality to gardens.

CONTAINERS AND COMPOST FOR BAMBOOS

Large pots, wooden tubs and square boxes create ideal homes for bamboos. Large, ornate, wide-based pots are ideal for low-growing bamboos, especially when positioned in an exotic garden. Large tubs and square boxes are better suited for tall-growing bamboos and are usually left in the same position until the soil is congested with roots. Garden soil often contains pests. Therefore, it is always best to use a combination of equal parts moisture-retentive peat-based soil and loam-based potting soil. Thoroughly mix them together before planting a bamboo.

BAMBOO CARE ...

- Stand the container out of direct sunlight and away from strong gusts of wind that dry the plants.
- Keep the soil moist – it may need watering several times a day during summer, especially if the weather is particularly hot.
- Brush snow from the leaves and canes before it freezes and becomes difficult to remove.
- If winters are especially severe, remember to wrap the container in sacking to prevent the soil freezing and damaging the roots.
- Repot any congested plants in spring. If necessary, plants can also be divided at the same time.

BAMBOOS FOR CONTAINERS

Low displays:
- *Pleioblastus pygmaeus*
- *Pleioblastus variegatus*
- *Pleioblastus viridistriatus*

Medium displays:
- *Fargesia murielae*
- *Phyllostachys nigra*
- *Thamnocalamus tesselatus*

Tall and dominant displays:
- *Fargesia nitida*
- *Phyllostachys aurea*
- *Pseudosasa japonica*
- *Semiarundinaria fastuosa*
- *Thamnocalamus spathiflorus*

Fargesia nitida
Fountain Bamboo (USA/UK)
Queen of the Arundinarias (USA/UK)
Height: 12–15 ft (3.6–4.5 m)
Spread: Clump-forming and non-invasive
Also known as *Arundinaria nitida* and *Sinarundinaria nitida*, it has bright green leaves and light purple canes.

Phyllostachys nigra
Black-stemmed Bamboo (USA/UK)
Black Bamboo (USA/UK)
Height: 8–10 ft (2.4–3 m)
Spread: Moderately invasive
Also known as *Sinarundinaria nigra*, it has dark green leaves and canes at first green but later jet-black.

Pleioblastus viridistriatus
Golden-haired Bamboo (USA/UK)
Height: 3–4 ft (90 cm–1.2 m)
Spread: Moderately invasive
Also known as *Arundinaria viridistriatus*, it has purple-green canes and golden-yellow leaves with pea-green stripes.

Pseudosasa japonica
Arrow Bamboo (USA/UK)
Metake (USA/UK)
Height: 8–15 ft (2.4–4.5 m)
Spread: Moderately invasive
Also known as *Arundinaria japonica*, it has sharply pointed, lance-shaped, dark glossy-green leaves.

Bonsai for patios

Bonsai is the ancient art of growing a tree in a shallow container and – by pruning leaves, shoots, roots and branches – encouraging it to remain small and healthy. These trees can be either deciduous (meaning they lose their leaves in winter) or evergreen. Some are grown for their attractive foliage, and others for their flowers or berries. They are outdoor plants and can be displayed on supports or staging on a patio throughout the year.

What is bonsai?

DISPLAYING OUTDOOR BONSAI

Bonsai are best viewed at about waist height, cascading ones perhaps slightly higher. Permanent staging – free-standing or attached to a wall – is one way to display plants, but it should not be in continual shade. Other ways are to use tall display stands on which cascading bonsai can be placed, or "monkey poles," which are small platforms at the tops of stout wooden or concrete supports. Wherever your bonsai plants are positioned, make certain that slugs and snails cannot reach them, but that you will have all-weather access to the plants right throughout the year.

DO BONSAI NEED REGULAR ATTENTION?

Bonsai need attention throughout the year, but especially during their growing period.
- Watering: regular watering is needed during spring, summer and into autumn. During winter, outdoor bonsai usually gain sufficient moisture from rain and, perhaps, snow. At the peak of summer, plants need to be watered several times a day. Allow the water to drain freely through the soil.
- Feeding: like all other plants, bonsai need to be fed regularly, although after being repotted wait until they are displaying active growth before applying fertilizers. From spring to early autumn apply a weak, general fertilizer. Use a proprietary bonsai fertilizer, and follow the instructions.

BONSAI FOR PATIOS

Deciduous trees:
- *Acer buergerianum*
- *Acer palmatum*
- *Fagus sylvatica*
- *Ulmus procera*
- *Zelkova serrata*

Flowering shrubs, trees and climbers:
- *Forsythia*
- *Malus baccata*
- *Wisteria floribunda*

Conifers:
- *Ginkgo biloba* (deciduous)
- *Pinus sylvestris* (evergreen)
- *Tsuga heterophylla* (evergreen)

Acer palmatum
Japanese Maple (USA/UK)
An elegant, graceful tree with five-lobed (occasionally seven) leaves, which are green at first but by autumn reveal purplish or bronze hues. It can be used in most bonsai styles and is especially attractive as a specimen or in a group.

Pinus parviflora
Japanese White Pine (USA/UK)
Also known as *Pinus pentaphylla*, this evergreen conifer develops a low crown and wide-spreading branches. The purple bark is attractive, with patches of black scales. The blue-white needles are borne in groups of five.

Salix babylonica
Weeping Willow (USA/UK)
Vigorous, fast-growing, graceful tree, initially with an upward nature and later revealing pendent branches bearing slender, narrow, lance-shaped, pale to mid-green leaves. It also displays greenish-yellow catkins.

Wisteria floribunda
Japanese Wisteria (USA/UK)
Well-known deciduous climber with slender branches and leaves each formed of 12–19 oval leaflets. The spectacular, violet-blue, fragrant flowers are borne during late spring and early summer. There is a white-flowered form.

Bulbous plants

How do I grow these plants?

Bulbs and corms are nature's powerhouses of reserved energy, and the range of them for growing in tubs, pots, window boxes, troughs and wall baskets is wide. They include diminutive types, such as Crocuses and miniature Daffodils, and Lilies in pots that flood patios with color and fragrance. For success, it is essential that healthy bulbs are used. Inferior bulbs will never create the spectacular displays that are essential for containers on a patio.

GROWING LILIES IN POTS

The range of Lilies for growing in pots is extensive. They can be planted at any time between mid-autumn and early spring. Basal-rooting types do best, however, when planted in autumn. Here is the way to plant them.

- As soon as the bulbs are available, plant them singly in 6–8 in (15–20 cm) wide pots. Use only a well-drained, soil-based soil.
- Place drainage material in the pot's base. Stem-rooting types are planted low down in the pot. A general clue is to plant all bulbs to about two and a half times their depth. *Lilium candidum*, however, should be planted with its nose just below the soil's surface.
- Water the soil and place the pots in a cool position: either plunge outdoors and cover with coarse sand, or place in a cool cellar or dark shed.
- When growth appears, gradually move the pots into better light and water to keep the soil evenly moist.

Lilies for growing in pots:
- *Lilium auratum* (Golden-rayed Lily): large, brilliant-white, bowl-shaped flowers during late summer and early autumn. Stem-rooting type.
- *Lilium candidum* (Madonna Lily): white, trumpet-shaped flowers with a honey-like fragrance and golden anthers in early and mid-summer. Basal-rooting type.
- *Lilium hansonii*: pale orange-yellow, fragrant, Turk's-cap shaped flowers with brown spots during early and mid-summer. Stem-rooting type.
- *Lilium longiflorum* (Easter Lily): white, trumpet-shaped flowers with golden pollen during mid- and late summer. Stem-rooting type.
- *Lilium speciosum*: fragrant, bowl-shaped, white flowers shaded crimson during late summer and into early autumn. A warm patio is essential; alternatively, grow it in a cool greenhouse. Stem-rooting type.

GETTING A BETTER DISPLAY FROM DAFFODILS

Plant Daffodil bulbs in early autumn for a feast of glorious and radiant color in spring.
- Clean and stand a tub in position. Form a 2 in (5 cm) thick layer of coarse drainage material in the base.
- Add and firm good-quality, loam-based soil to within 8 in (20 cm) of the tub's top.

- Space healthy, good-quality Daffodil bulbs about 3 in (7.5 cm) apart. Trickle and firm soil between them.
- Position a further layer of bulbs, with their bases between the ones already in position.
- Add and firm compost to within 1 in (2.5 cm) of the tub's rim. Gently but thoroughly water the soil.

Chionodoxa gigantea
Glory of the Snow (USA/UK)
Height: 8 in (20 cm)
Spread: 3–4 in (7.5–10 cm)
Pale violet-blue flowers, about 1½ in (36 mm) across, from late winter to mid-spring. Each flower has a white center.

Crocus chrysanthus hybrids
Crocus (USA/UK)
Height: 3–4 in (7.5–10 cm)
Spread: 2–3 in (5–7.5 cm)
Well-known cormous plants that produce cup-shaped, honey-scented flowers in many colors during late winter and early spring.

Galanthus nivalis
Common Snowdrop (USA/UK)
Height: 3–7 in (7.5–18 cm)
Spread: 3–5 in (7.5–13 cm)
Distinctive, with strap-like leaves and white flowers from mid-winter to early spring. 'Flore-plena' has double flowers.

Hyacinthus orientalis
Common Hyacinth (USA/UK)
Garden Hyacinth (USA/UK)
Height: 6–9 in (15–23 cm)
Spread: 4–6 in (10–15 cm)
Flower spires packed with flowers in a wide color range, including white, yellow, pink, red and blue, in spring.

Iris danfordiae
Miniature Iris (USA/UK)
Height: 4 in (10 cm)
Spread: 3–4 in (7.5–10 cm)
Honey-scented, lemon-yellow flowers, up to 3 in (7.5 cm) wide, during mid- and late winter.

Muscari armeniacum
Grape Hyacinth (USA/UK)
Height: 8–10 in (20–25 cm)
Spread: 3–4 in (7.5–10 cm)
Clump-forming, with narrow, green leaves and upright stems bearing azure-blue flowers during mid- and late spring.

Narcissus bulbocodium
Hoop Petticoat Daffodil (USA/UK)
Height: 3–5 in (7.5–13 cm)
Spread: 3 in (7.5 cm)
Bulbous, with distinctive, yellow, 1 in (2.5 cm) long, funnel-shaped flowers during late winter and early spring.

Narcissus – Trumpet types
Daffodil (USA/UK)
Height: 13–18 in (32–45 cm)
Spread: 3–4 in (7.5–10 cm)
Popular bulbous plants, with distinctive trumpet-like flowers in yellow or white outdoors during spring.

BULB "FACTS OF LIFE"

- Always buy good-quality bulbs for planting in containers. Some large-flowered Daffodil bulbs are sold for naturalizing in grass, but these are not suitable for containers.
- Don't reuse in outdoor containers any bulbs that earlier were forced into early flower indoors. These bulbs are best naturalized around shrubs in borders.
- Don't mix different Lily bulbs when using large containers, such as tubs.
- Don't mix different varieties of Hyacinths in the same container, as they may not all flower at the same time and the dramatic nature of the display will be diminished.

OTHER BULBS TO CONSIDER ...

- *Anemone blanda* (Spring-flowering Windflower): blue flowers from late winter to mid-spring.
- *Chionodoxa luciliae* (Glory of the Snow): blue, white-centered flowers during late winter and early spring.
- *Eranthis hyemalis* (Winter Aconite): lemon-yellow flowers during late winter and early spring.
- *Ipheion uniflora*: white to deep blue flowers in spring.
- *Iris reticulata*: deep purple-blue, with orange blazes, during late winter and early spring.
- *Leucojum vernum* (Snowflake): white, in late winter and early spring.
- *Tulipa fosteriana*: scarlet, in mid-spring.

Tulipa greigii
Height: 9–12 in (23–30 cm)
Spread: 5–6 in (13–15 cm)
Hardy species Tulip that produces blunt-pointed, orange-scarlet flowers during mid-spring.

Tulips – Single Early
Height: 6–15 in (15–38 cm)
Spread: 4–5 in (10–13 cm)
Select short types for containers. Wide color range for flowers during mid-spring. Flowers often open flat. Double Early Tulips (illustrated above) can also be grown in containers; use short types to avoid wind damage.

Culinary herbs for patios

How can I grow herbs on a patio?

There are many containers which can be used to grow herbs on patios, including grow bags. Window boxes are ideal homes for small herbs (see below), while pots and planters are other solutions to having culinary herbs within easy reach of a kitchen. Unlike when grown in herb gardens in borders – where plants can be left undisturbed for several years – be prepared to check plants in containers regularly, and to remove invasive types.

HARVESTING AND STORING CULINARY HERBS

All herbs are better for being used fresh, but there are several months when picking is not possible for some plants.

- Herbs can be dried or frozen for winter use (as such, they will be unsuitable as a garnish). However, remember that the flavor of dried herbs becomes intensified, and you will need only half the quantity compared to fresh herbs.
- When freezing herbs, pick and put them in plastic bags and place in rigid containers to prevent them being squashed when in a freezer. The most suitable ones for freezing are Mint, Chives and Parsley.

GROWING HERBS IN WINDOW BOXES

Window boxes in summer are ideal homes for small herbs. In the cycle of using window boxes, one planted with herbs can be put in place immediately the spring-flowering display has been removed (see page 52 for details of using window boxes).

Although herbs can be planted directly into compost in a window box, it is usually better to leave them in individual pots and to position them directly in a window box; pack moist peat around them. Invasive herbs such as Mint are then kept under control. Additionally, herbs which cease to be attractive can be removed and young plants put in their place.

GROWING HERBS IN POTS

No patio is complete without a few pots of herbs near the kitchen door.

- Groups of ornamental pots, as well as more functional types, are ideal homes for herbs, from Chives and Mint to Parsley and Thyme.
- Most of these herbs can be left in pots and other containers for several years, but Parsley is usually grown as an annual and fresh plants will need to be raised each year.
- Bay trees are often grown as half-standards in tubs or large pots. Always use large containers and potting soil; this gives the plant a stable base.

Allium schoenoprasum
Chives
Height: 6–9 in (15–23 cm)
Spread: 8–10 in (20–25 cm)
Bulbous, hardy perennial with grass-like, tubular leaves with a mild onion-like flavor, and starry flowers.

Laurus nobilis
Bay
Height: 4–6 ft (1.2–1.8 m) in a tub
Spread: 2–2½ ft (60–75 cm) in a tub
Hardy evergreen tree; ideal as a half-standard in a tub. The glossy, mid-green leaves are aromatic and added to food.

Melissa officinalis
Balm
Height: 1½–2 ft (45–60 cm) in a tub
Spread: 12–18 in (30–45 cm) in a tub
Herbaceous perennial, ideal for a tub. The leaves have a refreshing lemon scent and are ideal for flavoring drinks.

Mentha spicata
Mint – Common Mint or Spearmint
Height: 12–18 in (30–45 cm)
Spread: Invasive
Herbaceous perennial with aromatic leaves which have a distinctive spearmint flavor; used in mint sauce.

Origanum majorana
Marjoram
Height: 1½–2 ft (45–60 cm)
Spread: 12–15 in (30–38 cm)
Bushy, slightly tender perennial known as Sweet or Knotted Marjoram. Sweetly aromatic leaves.

Petroselinum crispum
Parsley
Height: 12–18 in (30–45 cm)
Spread: 9–15 in (23–38 cm)
Hardy biennial that is invariably grown as an annual, with branching stems bearing mid-green leaves; it is used to flavor and garnish.

Rosmarinus officinalis
Rosemary
Height: 3–4 ft (90 cm–1.2 m) in a tub
Spread: 1½–2½ ft (45–75 cm) in a tub
Hardy, evergreen shrub with aromatic leaves. Mauve, white or bright blue flowers during late spring and summer.

Ruta graveolens
Rue
Height: 12–18 in (30–45 cm) in a pot
Spread: 12–15 in (30–38 cm) in a pot
Hardy, evergreen shrub with deeply divided, blue-green leaves. When picked and chopped they are added to salads.

Salvia officinalis
Sage
Height: 1–1½ ft (30–45 cm) in a tub
Spread: 1–1½ ft (30–45 cm) in a tub
Evergreen, slightly tender shrub with gray-green, wrinkled leaves that produces violet-blue flowers during early and mid-summer.

Thymus vulgaris
Thyme – Common Thyme
Height: 4–8 in (10–20 cm)
Spread: 9–12 in (23–30 cm)
Hardy, low-growing evergreen shrub with aromatic, dark green leaves that are added to flavor food and stuffings.

HERBS IN PLANTERS

Growing herbs in planters – containers with cupped holes around their sides – is ideal for collections of small herbs in a small area. The range of their shapes and colors will create both an attractive feature and a supply of culinary herbs throughout summer.

- Some planters are formed of plastic and others of fiberglass and reconstituted stone.
- Because plants are usually left in the planter for several years, ensure that excess water can easily escape from the planter's base, and that a loam-based soil is used.
- To keep invasive herbs small, regularly nip off their growing tips.

AROMATIC THYMES

In addition to the Common Thyme (*Thymus vulgaris*) with its aromatic leaves, others have attention-seeking bouquets. Here are two of them:

- Caraway-scented Thyme (*Thymus herba-barona*): sometimes known as the Seed-cake Thyme, it has caraway-scented, matte-green leaves borne on plants with a prostrate nature. Tubular, pale-lilac flowers appear in terminal clusters in early summer.
- Lemon-scented Thyme (*Thymus x citriodorus*): with an appearance similar to Common Thyme, it has lemon-scented leaves. For extra color, try the colored or variegated-leaved forms. It is used in the same way as Common Thyme.

AROMATIC MINTS

- Apple Mint (*Mentha rotundifolia* or *Mentha suaveolens*): sometimes known as the Round Leaf Mint, it has pale green leaves that emit the fragrance of apples.
- Brandy Mint (*Mentha x piperita*): spear-like to heart-shaped green leaves that are often tinged reddish-purple and that have a strong peppermint redolence.
- Ginger Mint (*Mentha x gracilis*; also known as *Mentha x gentilis*): mid-green leaves that have the redolence of ginger.
- Peppermint Mint (*Mentha requienii*): also known as the Corsican Mint and Crème de Menthe Mint, it has pale green leaves with a peppermint scent.

Climbing plants

Can climbers be grown in containers?

It is possible to grow a wide range of climbers in containers and to create magnificent displays. These plants include perennial climbers, annual climbers and herbaceous types. Some of these, such as Clematis and Wisteria, are famed for their flowers, and others for their colorful foliage. Many are also superbly fragrant. However, when climbers are grown in containers they need regular attention to ensure that the soil is evenly moist throughout summer.

SUITABLE CONTAINERS FOR CLIMBERS

For climbers that remain in the same container for several years, it is essential that the container holds as much soil as possible. The larger the amount of soil, the less the roots are at risk from overheating during summer and freezing in winter. Additionally, wooden containers, with their ability to thermally insulate soil, are better than metal types which heat up quickly in summer and remain cold in winter. Large earthenware pots are ideal for climbers. If the container is large, always put it in position before filling it with soil, or you may not be able to move it.

CREATING TRIPOD DISPLAYS

Instead of creating a screen-like display of flowers and leaves against a trellis, try a tripod display. This is ideal for producing a display that can be viewed from all sides. Suitable climbers for this include half-hardy annuals and the herbaceous *Humulus lupulus* 'Aureus' (Yellow-leaved Hop).

- Use a large tub and insert 4–5 5–6 ft (1.5–1.8 m) long bamboo canes into soil at the edge of a tub.
- Angle their tops towards the center and tie them together, about 6 in (15 cm) from the top.
- Use several plants if you want to create a quick display.

THREE STUNNING DISPLAYS TO TRY...

- Put three plants of the spectacular *Clematis macropetala* in the top of an old, upright, wooden barrel. Ensure the barrel is well drained and use potting soil. In late spring and early summer it will clothe the barrel with 2–3 in (5–7.5 cm) wide, light and dark blue flowers.
- Position a tub or a large terracotta pot alongside ornate railings and plant a large-flowered Clematis in it. There are many to choose from, and it will drench the railings in color.
- Construct a teepee of bamboo canes in a tub and plant several plants of the delightfully fragrant Sweet Pea in it to grow up the canes.

Cobaea scandens
Cathedral Bells (UK)
Cup-and-Saucer Vine (USA/UK)
Height: 6 ft (1.8 m) in a container
Half-hardy perennial usually grown as a half-hardy annual. It produces purple-green flowers throughout summer.

Eccremocarpus scaber
Chilean Glory Flower (UK)
Glory Flower (USA)
Height: 6 ft (1.8 m) in a container
Slightly tender (in temperate climates) evergreen climber. Tubular, orange-scarlet flowers are borne throughout summer.

Humulus lupulus 'Aureus'
Yellow European Hop (USA)
Yellow-leaved Hop (USA/UK)
Height: 5–6 ft (1.5–1.8 m) – in a container
Hardy herbaceous perennial with scrambling stems bearing masses of five-lobed, bright yellowish-green leaves.

Ipomoea tricolor
Morning Glory (USA/UK)
Height: 5–6 ft (1.5–1.6 m) in a container
Half-hardy annual with large, trumpet-shaped flowers in blue or purple during late summer and into autumn.

GROWING SWEET PEAS

Lathyrus odoratus (Sweet Pea) is a well-known climber, with masses of flowers in many colors throughout summer. Colors include shades of red, blue, pink and purple, as well as white.

- The Sweet Pea is really a hardy annual, but to produce quick displays in containers it is invariably grown as a half-hardy annual.
- Seeds are sown in gentle warmth in a greenhouse early in the year, for planting into containers as soon as all risk of frost has passed.
- For growing in pots, always choose dwarf varieties of Sweet Pea.
- Regularly pick the flowers to encourage further ones to develop.

Lathyrus odoratus
Sweet Pea (USA/UK)
Height: 2–6 ft (60 cm–1.8 m) in a container
Hardy annual usually grown as a half-hardy annual. Wide range of scented flowers from early summer to autumn.

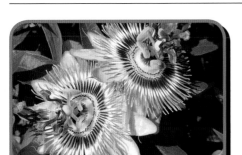

Passiflora caerulea
Blue Passion Flower (UK)
Common Passion Flower (UK)
Height: 6–8 ft (1.8–2.4 m) in a container
Slightly tender scrambling deciduous climber with 3 in (7.5 cm) wide, white flowers with blue centers from early to late summer.

Thunbergia alata
Black-eyed Susan (UK)
Black-eyed Susan Vine (USA)
Height: 4–6 ft (1.2–1.8 m) in a container
Hardy annual climber with orange-yellow, 2 in (5 cm) wide flowers with dark centers produced from early summer through to autumn.

Tropaeolum majus
Garden Nasturtium (USA)
Nasturtium (UK)
Height: 5–6 ft (1.5–1.8 m) in a container
Hardy annual (some climbing, others low and trailing) with flowers in many colors throughout summer.

Tropaeolum perigrinum
Canary Creeper (USA/UK)
Canary Bird Flower (USA)
Height: 5–6 ft (1.5–1.8 m) in a container
Half-hardy perennial that is usually grown as a hardy annual. Irregularly shaped yellow flowers appear from mid-summer to autumn.

CLEMATIS FOR CONTAINERS

Clematis will create dramatic feasts of color, but can be difficult to grow in a container, usually because it is too small and does not hold sufficient soil to provide a reserve of moisture. If these problems can be overcome, however, the following are possible patio brighteners.

- *Clematis armandii*: evergreen climber with saucer-shaped, 2–2½ in (5–6.5 cm) wide, white flowers in mid-spring, sometimes slightly later. The form 'Apple Blossom' has pink and white flowers, while 'Snowdrift' produces pure white flowers. It is vigorous and needs a large structure up which to climb.
- *Clematis florida* 'Sieboldii': usually deciduous, but in warm climates is semi-evergreen, with a shrubby and sparse habit. During mid- and late spring it bears white, double flowers.
- Clematis – large-flowered types: these are popular clematis but not always successful unless the compost remains cool and moist. Many superb varieties and colors. Rather than providing special supports, position the container near an ornamental wrought-iron fence.
- *Clematis macrocarpa*: during late spring and early summer it displays 2–3 in (5–7.5 cm) wide, light and dark blue flowers. See far left for growing it in a large barrel.

GROWING WISTERIA IN A POT

Wisteria is a woody, deciduous climber that normally grows against a wall, where it produces pendulous clusters of fragrant, violet-blue flowers during late spring and early summer. Use *Wisteria floribunda* (Japanese Wisteria), which is not as vigorous as *Wisteria sinensis* (Chinese Wisteria). In addition to the ordinary blue-flowered type, there is a white form. It can also be grown in a tub or large terracotta pot on a wind-sheltered patio. Train a single stem upwards to create a canopy at head height. Support the stem, as well as providing a framework of wires for the laterally trained branches. Both winter and summer pruning will be necessary to prevent excessive growth.

Plants for vestibules and porches

How do I grow these plants?

Vestibules and porches are halfway homes between outdoors and indoors, and provide good conditions for growing frost-tender indoor plants. Vestibules are enclosed areas, but porches tend to be more exposed to outdoor weather – especially those that are completely open in design, without any kind of outer door. Indoor hanging baskets (with drip-trays to prevent water spilling on floors) enable a wide range of foliage and flowering plants to be grown in these areas.

PLANTING TECHNIQUES

There are two main ways of growing plants in indoor hanging baskets. The first method involves removing their growing pots and planting a group of plants in soil, while the other way is to leave them in their pots and just to place them in a flat-based hanging basket. The latter method enables plants to be easily swapped and those not looking attractive to be removed. The techniques of these methods are described and illustrated on page 57. Whichever method is chosen, ensure that the soil is evenly moist, especially during summer. In winter, it can be kept slightly drier.

FERNS FOR VESTIBULES AND PORCHES

In addition to "proper" ferns, there are others that have a similar appearance and often have the word "fern" in their common name. Here is a selection of ferns and their "lookalikes."

- *Asparagus densiflorus* 'Myersii' (Foxtail Fern): upright, then arching, bottlebrush-like stems bearing mid-green leaves. Minimum winter temperature 45°F (7°C). Either plant it in a hanging basket or position it in a wall bracket.
- *Asparagus densiflorus* 'Sprengeri' (Emerald Fern): arching, wiry stems bearing mid-green leaves. Minimum winter temperature 45°F (7°C). Plant in a hanging basket or position in a wall bracket.
- *Asplenium bulbiferum* (Mother Fern): large, finely cut fronds with small bulbils that weigh them down. Minimum winter temperature 39°F (4°C). Plant in a hanging basket or position in a wall bracket.
- *Nephrolepis exaltata* (Ladder Fern or Sword Fern): upright and cascading, deeply divided, sword-like fronds. 'Bostoniensis' has more arching fronds and 'Marshallii' develops pale green, densely crested fronds. Minimum winter temperature 45–50°F (7–10°C). Avoid drafts, and plant in a hanging basket.
- *Pellaea rotundifolia* (Button Fern): unusual fern, with small, button-like, leathery fronds on wiry stems.

Begonia x tuberhybrida 'Pendula'
Trailing Tuberous-rooted Begonia (UK)
Height: 6–8 in (15–20 cm)
Trailing: 12–15 in (30–38 cm)
Tender, tuberous-rooted plant with rose-like summer flowers in many colors.

Campanula isophylla 'Krystal' varieties
Star of Bethlehem (USA/UK)
Height: 6 in (15 cm)
Trailing: to 18 in (45 cm)
Hardy perennial with masses of star-shaped, blue or white flowers, 1 in (25 mm) wide, from early to late summer.

Chlorophytum comosum 'Variegatum'
Spider Plant (USA/UK)
Height: 8–12 in (20–30 cm)
Spread: 18–24 in (45–60 cm)
Tender houseplant with long, narrow, variegated leaves and long stems that produce plantlets at their ends.

Chrysanthemum morifolium – Cascade Types
Cascade Chrysanthemum (USA/UK)
Height: 4–6 in (10–15 cm)
Trailing: 12–18 in (30–45 cm) or more
Frost-tender plants with a trailing nature and small, daisy-like flowers, each about 1 in (2.5 cm) wide, in many colors.

VESTIBULE PLANTS FOR WALL BRACKETS

Some small, relatively hardy house-plants are ideal for positioning on their own in wall brackets – but avoid places where the temperature falls below 41°F (5°C). Here is a selection.

- *Callisia elegans* (Striped Inch Plant): fleshy, dull green leaves with white stripes and purple undersides.
- *Chlorophytum comosum* 'Variegatum': popular houseplant with long, narrow leaves that display white and green stripes. It produces plantlets at the ends of long stems.
- *Ficus radicans* 'Variegata' (Variegated Trailing Fig): cascading, wiry stems and lance-shaped, slender-pointed, mid-green leaves with creamy edges.
- *Oplismenus hirtellus* 'Variegatus' (Variegated Basket Vine): it creates a mass of tumbling stems bearing white-and-pink striped leaves.
- *Stenotaphrum secundatum* 'Variegatum' (Variegated Buffalo Grass): long, narrow, green leaves, up to 5 in (13 cm) long, banded in white.
- *Tolmiea menziesii* (Pig-a-back Plant, Thousand Mothers or Youth-on-age): elliptic to oval leaves, about 2 in (5 cm) long, striped in cream. There are several other forms, some of which are striped in silver.
- *Zebrina pendula* (Silvery Inch Plant): also known as *Tradescantia zebrina*, it has thick stems bearing mid-green leaves with two silvery bands on their upper surfaces.

Helichrysum petiolare
Licorice Plant (USA)
Height: 12–15 in (30–38 cm)
Spread: 18–20 in (45–50 cm) or more
Tender, shrubby perennial with lax, silvery-gray stems and leaves. There are several forms with variegated or colored leaves.

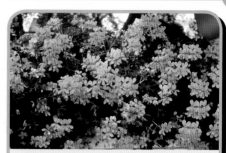

Pelargoniums –
Continental Geraniums
Balcon and Cascade Geraniums
Height: 8–12 in (20–30 cm)
Trailing and cascading
Frost-tender plants with masses of flowers throughout summer. Wide color range. Buy established plants.

Pelargonium peltatum
Hanging Geranium (USA)
Ivy-leaved Geranium (UK)
Height: 4–6 in (10–15 cm)
Trailing: 18 in (45 cm) or more
Tender perennial, with fleshy mid-green, ivy-shaped leaves. Carmine-pink flowers in summer. Several superb varieties.

MEDLEYS OF PLANTS FOR HANGING BASKETS

Using several different plants in a hanging basket creates long displays and with more varied interest.

- For a cool vestibule: a central *Calceolaria* x *herbeohybrida* (Pouch Flower) with trailing Petunias and Lobelias creates a colorful display in summer. By using yellow and blue, the display is ideal for positioning in a white-walled porch or vestibule.
- For a warm vestibule: position a Dracaena in the center, with trailing ivy-leaved *Pelargonium* (Geraniums) and Lobelias around it. A variation is to use a *Begonia* x *tuberhybrida* instead of the Dracaena.
- For an all-green display: flowering plants are not essential to hanging basket displays. Try a mixture of *Asparagus densiflorus* (Asparagus Fern) positioned in the center, surrounded by variegated small-leaved *Hedera helix* (Ivies), *Tradescantia zebrina* (Silvery Inch Plant; also known as *Zebrina pendula*) and *Sedum sieboldii* 'Medio-variegatum (Variegated Siebold's Stonecrop). This arrangement is highlighted when positioned against a white wall.
- For a color-packed display: plant a pink-flowered *Begonia* 'Gloire de Lorraine' in the center, with trailing variegated small-leaved *Hedera helix* (Ivies), cascading Fuchsias and trailing *Begonia* x *tuberhybrida* 'Pendula' (Basket Begonia).

Pericallis x *hybrida*
Florist's Cineraria (USA/UK)
Height: 12–15 in (30–38 cm)
Spread: 10–15 in (25–38 cm)
Half-hardy perennial, also known as *Senecio hybridus* and *Senecio cruentus*. Domed heads in many colors. Replace plants as necessary.

Saxifraga stolonifera
'Tricolor'
Strawberry Geranium (USA/UK)
Height: 4–6 in (10–15 cm)
Trailing: 12–18 in (30–45 cm), or more
Frost-tender plant with large, green leaves variegated pink and pale yellow. Use on its own or with other plants.

Growing vegetables in containers

Can I grow vegetables in containers?

Several vegetables can be grown in containers on a patio, and the most successful types are those cultivated for their leaves, pods or fruits (tomatoes). A few root crops, such as radishes, are possible in tubs, grow bags and window boxes, while carrots and beetroots can be put in deep boxes of friable compost. Large vegetables are best reserved for vegetable plots in a garden. Grow potatoes in grow bags, deep pots and tubs (see right).

SELECTING THE RIGHT CONTAINER

To gardeners with a large vegetable plot in a garden, food plants in containers on a patio are superfluous. Yet where balconies, courtyards and patios are the only gardening areas the thought of fresh vegetables is magnetic in its appeal. It is essential to match the vegetable to a container, and suitable partnerships are suggested on these pages. Slugs and snails are the major pests, but this risk can be reduced by putting ground-level containers on bricks. Grow bags can be placed on old, cut-down pallet bases sitting on four bricks. This also makes it easier to reposition the bags, if necessary.

TOMATOES IN HANGING BASKETS

- Line a 18 in (45 cm) wide wire-framed basket with black plastic.
- When all risk of frost has passed, plant 2–3 tomato plants in a basket. Partly fill the basket with loam-based soil; it produces shorter plants than peat-based types.
- Use a variety such as 'Tumbler,' 'Balconi Yellow' and 'Balconi Red.' Firm soil around the plants and trim the plastic slightly above the basket's edge. Additionally, use a knife to slit holes in the base to enable water to drain away.
- Plants are naturally bushy and do not need to have side shoots removed. Pick fruits as soon as they color.

VEGETABLES IN WINDOW BOXES

A wider range of vegetables can be grown in window boxes than in hanging baskets:

- Cucumbers: buy young plants as soon as all risk of frost has passed and plant one in the center of the window box. Pinch out the growing point when the plant has 6–7 leaves. Shoots can be left to trail.
- Sweet peppers: when all risk of frost has passed, put 2–3 young plants in a window box.
- Tomatoes: put two bush-type tomato plants in a window box as soon as all risk of frost has passed. It is not necessary to remove side shoots.

THOMPSON & MORGAN

Eggplants (Aubergines)
These frost-tender plants can be grown outdoors on warm patios. Fertile soil is essential. Harvest the fruits when they have an even color and are still glossy.

Grow in: Grow bags, large pots, wall baskets, troughs.

THOMPSON & MORGAN

Beans – bush type
These do not need supports and produce masses of bean pods on low-growing plants. Full sun and moisture-retentive soil are essential. Pick the beans while they are small and tender.

Grow in: grow bags, large pots.

THOMPSON & MORGAN

Zucchini (Courgettes)
They resemble small squash. These frost-tender plants can be grown outdoors on warm patios. Grow in fertile compost. Harvest the fruits when they are still young and small.

Grow in: grow bags, wall baskets, troughs.

THOMPSON & MORGAN

Cucumbers
Compact, bush-like varieties are essential and can be harvested within two months of being planted. Position them 10–12 in (25–30 cm) apart.

Grow in: grow bags, window boxes, wall baskets, troughs.

POTATOES IN TUBS

Tubs and large pots can be used to grow new potatoes.

- In early spring, thoroughly clean the container and check that there are drainage holes in its base. Place the container in position and raise it up on bricks.
- Form a 4–5 in (10–13 cm) thick layer of loam-based soil in the base and place 4–5 seed potatoes on top.
- Cover them with 4–5 in (10–13 cm) of soil. As shoots develop, cover them with further soil until within 1½ in (36 mm) of the rim.
- Keep the soil moist but not waterlogged and harvest them about three months later.

Lettuces

Choose small varieties and in a grow bag grow eight plants. Loose-leaf types are best and over a long period a few leaves can be removed at one time.

Grow in: grow bags.

Potatoes

Choose "first early" varieties and plant in mid-spring for a mid-summer crop. Alternatively, plant in mid-summer for an early-winter crop, but protection against frost is essential.

Grow in: tubs, large pots, special potato-growing containers, grow bags.

Radishes

Treat these rapid-growing vegetables as a space filler in containers where vegetables are being grown. Sow seeds in a succession from mid-spring to mid-summer; harvest the radishes when they are still young.

Grow in: tubs, window boxes, grow bags.

Sweet peppers

Also known as capsicums, these tender vegetables need fertile soil and plenty of sun and water in order to thrive. Do not plant outdoors until all risk of frost has passed.

Grow in: grow bags, wall baskets, troughs, window boxes.

Tomatoes

Popular frost-tender plants – a warm, wind-sheltered position is essential. Use cordon types (single, upright stem) in pots, but remember that bush types are much easier to grow.

Grow in: cordon types – pots; bush types – hanging baskets, wall baskets, troughs.

ADVANTAGES OF GROW BAGS

As well as being relatively inexpensive to buy, grow bags have several other advantages:

- They are lightweight and therefore ideal for use on balconies, as well as on patios and terraces;
- The soil is clean and free from all pests and diseases;
- They are easily transported home and stored before use;
- Good growth is possible, provided that plants are fed regularly once they have become established;
- They have a variety of uses, ranging from vegetables to herbs. The bags can even be recycled for further use during the following year.

PREPARING A GROW BAG FOR USE

For success with a grow bag, spend some time in its preparation.

- Clean the outside, then shake to loosen the soil; place it on a flat, level surface.
- If slugs and snails are likely to be a problem, place the bag on a board slightly raised above the ground.
- Sometimes there is a central band which prevents the sides splaying apart.
- Pierce a number of drainage holes, as indicated on the bag.
- Before putting plants into the bag, saturate the soil with water and allow it to drain.

VEGETABLES IN GROW BAGS

The number of plants refer to a standard grow bag.

- Bush French beans: plant six bushy plants. Pods are ready to be harvested when they snap when bent – about 4–6 in (10–15 cm) long.
- Zucchinis: use two plants. Water and feed regularly and as soon as the fruits are young and tender, harvest them. This encourages the development of further zucchinis.
- Lettuces: grow eight lettuces in a bag.
- Tomatoes: plant 3–4 young plants. Supports are essential (proprietary types are available). Regularly water and feed plants.

Growing fruit in containers

Can I grow fruit in containers?

Several types of fruit can be grown in containers, but they are longer-lived than vegetables and therefore require more care and attention from one year to another. The majority of container-grown fruits need large containers, such as tubs and large pots. Strawberries, however, can be grown in hanging baskets and planters, as well as in large barrels with planting holes cut in their sides, a traditional method dating back more than a hundred years.

ASPECT AND CARE

A warm, wind-sheltered position is essential, as well as regularly and thoroughly watering the soil throughout summer. Good drainage is vital, and always use loam-based soil rather than peat-based types. In winter, use plastic or two large tiles angled like a tent over the soil to prevent it becoming too wet; this causes root decay as well as putting them at risk from frozen soil. Birds soon damage buds and fruits if they are not prevented by the use of netting. Preferably, a wire-netting cage is best, but this is an expensive way to protect your fruits.

STRAWBERRIES IN HANGING BASKETS

Strawberries do not need a large amount of soil, and as well as being planted in hanging baskets do well in other soil-restricted containers such as window boxes and wall baskets.

- Use a seed-raised variety and buy young plants in late spring or early summer, when all risk of frost has passed. If there is a risk of frost after being planted, place a few sheets of newspaper over them.
- Put three plants in a large hanging basket, or about 8 in (20 cm) apart in window boxes and wall baskets.

STRAWBERRIES IN PLANTERS

Some planters – with holes in their sides – are made of fiberglass, others of reconstituted stone. Whatever the material, they create ideal homes for strawberry plants, which can be left in position for 2–3 years before replanting is needed.

- Check that drainage holes in the base are not blocked. Then, place 2 in (5 cm) of coarse drainage material in the base.
- Roll a piece of wire-netting (slightly less in length than the depth of the planter) into a tube about 3 in (7.5 cm) wide. Place it vertically in the planter's base and fill with large stones.
- Fill the planter with loam-based soil to level with the first planting hole.
- Put a strawberry plant in the hole, with its roots spread out on the soil, and add and firm further soil.
- Add more soil and, in stages, both plant the container and fill with soil.
- Put strawberry plants in the top. Lightly but thoroughly water the soil.
- Several varieties can be used, including 'Bounty' (mid-summer fruiting), 'Cambridge Favorite' (early and mid-summer fruiting) and 'Gento' (fruiting in late summer and into autumn).

STRAWBERRIES IN BARRELS AND CASKS

Wooden barrels, with their traditional shape and rustic nature, have long been used to decoratively and productively grow strawberries. Large, waist-high barrels, earlier used to transport wine, can be modified and used to create eye-catching features on a patio. Converting a large barrel is described on page 71.

- Casks – usually about knee height – can also be modified, either with holes cut in their sides or just with one end taken out, the cask turned upright and strawberry plants inserted in the top.
- Whether strawberries are planted in barrels or casks, good drainage is essential to prevent their roots becoming damaged.

Apples
If there is only space for one "tree" fruit, choose an apple. The best way is to buy a "family" tree and to grow as a pyramid. Picking and eating times depend on the variety (as indicated on page 49).

Blueberries
These low-growing bush fruits are increasingly popular and easy to grow. Birds can be a problem when fruits start to ripen, but netting will keep them at bay. Using both ericaceous soil and soft water is essential.

APPLES IN TUBS AND LARGE POTS

Apples are a popular tree fruit to grow in a container, but there are a few vital considerations to bear in mind.

- Wooden tubs or large terracotta pots are essential, at least 15 in (38 cm) deep and across. Place broken pieces of clay pots in them to create good drainage; use potting soil.
- Use dwarfing rootstocks such as M27 or M9. Without their use, growing apples in pots is not practical.
- To ensure pollination (and the subsequent development of fruit) choose a "family" tree, where 3–4 different yet compatible varieties have been grafted onto one rootstock. Alternatively, it is necessary to plant – in separate pots – several varieties.
- Buy a two-year-old tree and plant and stake it.
- It is best trained as a pyramid, which means in winter cutting back the leading shoot to about 6 in (15 cm) from where it developed from the trunk. Additionally, cut back side shoots near the plant's top to 6–8 in (15–20 cm) from the trunk, and those near the base to 10–12 in (25–30 cm) from the trunk.
- During the second winter, cut back all branches to about 6–8 in (15–20 cm) from where they developed during the previous growing period.
- During the first year, allow 2–3 fruits to develop; in later years, expect about 10 lb (4.5 kg) of fruit.

Varieties to try include:

- 'Blenheim Orange': dessert and culinary variety; pick apples in mid-autumn; they are ready for eating in late autumn and early winter.
- 'Discovery': dessert variety; pick apples in late summer; they will be ready for eating during late summer and early autumn.
- 'Egremont Russet': dessert variety; pick apples in early autumn; they will be ready for eating from mid-autumn to early winter.
- 'James Grieve': dessert variety; pick apples in early autumn, ready for eating in early and mid-autumn.
- 'Sunset': dessert variety; pick apples in early autumn, ready for eating from mid-autumn to early winter.

Figs

Figs require a warm climate and a sheltered position. Embryonic fruits develop in the summer and are harvested during the following year. A fig is ready for picking when the stalk weakens and the fruit hangs freely.

Peaches

A warm position is essential for peaches. Test each fruit individually for picking; cup each one in the palm of your hand and twist – if the stalk easily parts from the branch, this means that the fruit is ready.

Strawberries

Strawberries are the most popular fruits for growing in a variety of containers, from hanging baskets to planters and barrels. Regularly check fruits for picking. This should be done in the morning, when they are dry and have colored all over.

PEACHES IN LARGE POTS

Apart from shelter from cold wind, there are a few other essentials:

- Position in the warmth of a sun-drenched wall.
- For ease of pruning, grow as a bush.
- Use a dwarfing rootstock such as Pixy. It produces a tree 6–7 ft (1.8–2.1 m) high in a tub or large pot.
- Select a relatively hardy variety, such as 'Duke of York' (for picking mid-summer) or 'Peregrine' (for picking during late summer).
- Protect flowers in spring from frost and birds, and later protect the ripening fruits from birds.
- It is essential that you hand-pollinate the flowers.

FIGS IN LARGE POTS

Unless their roots are constricted, figs are rampant and produce leafy growth at the expense of fruits. Therefore, they are ideal for growing in containers. Here are a few essentials for success.

- In spring, put a young fig plant in a large tub and position in the shelter and warmth of a wall.
- Grow the fig as a small bush (rather than as a fan).
- During winter, protect shoots and young figs from frost.
- Repot plants every 2–3 years.
- Select varieties such as 'Brown Turkey' (for picking late summer and early autumn) and 'White Marseilles' (for picking late summer and early autumn).

BLUEBERRIES IN LARGE POTS

These are increasingly popular and easy to grow in large containers. Here are a few clues to success with them.

- Choose a tub or large wooden box at least 1½ ft (45 cm) deep and wide. Good drainage is essential.
- Use ericaceous (acid) soil and plant in spring. They grow to about 4 ft (1.2 m) high.
- Use the popular and widely grown variety 'Bluecrop.'
- Attractive white flowers, tinged with pink, appear in spring, and fruits follow in mid-summer.
- Protect fruits from birds and, preferably, water with rainwater.

Choosing and buying plants

Much of the success of growing plants in containers – as well as in gardens – is to buy healthy, well-established, pest-and-disease-free plants that will quickly become established and create magnificent displays. Summer-flowering bedding plants especially have a limited time to become established before they are expected to drench containers in color. The selection of bulbs for spring display also needs care; inferior bulbs never produce good displays.

A small, decorative, terracotta trough introduces extra color and interest to a patio or to a gravel path like this one.

WHERE TO BUY PLANTS

Many places sell plants for putting in containers, and these include garden centers, nurseries, supermarkets and local shops. There are also garden clubs and stalls in markets, and plants can be purchased by mail order. Wherever you obtain your plants, however, buy only the best quality – an inexpensive buy is a costly experience if it does not produce a good display several months later.

Garden centers

Buying from garden centers is popular and plants can be checked before you buy. Additionally, advice is often possible if you are in doubt about what to buy. They usually have a wide range of plants which are inspected daily to ensure they are healthy and attractive.

Nurseries

Plants bought from nurseries have usually been grown on that site and their qualities and attributes are well known to the nursery staff. For that reason, advice is usually available. Some nurseries specialize in specific plants, such as bamboos, trees and shrubs, while others have a general range of plants.

Mail order

This is an ideal way to buy plants if you are housebound or have transportation difficulties. Plants are advertised in national and local newspapers, and glossy magazines. For quality, it is necessary to rely on the integrity of the supplier. Check plants immediately after delivery and notify suppliers of any problems.

WHAT TO LOOK FOR

GOOD HEALTH

Before buying any plant, check that it is growing strongly and looks bright and healthy. Here are a few clues when inspecting plants:

- Soil should be moist but not waterlogged. Plants can wilt from having dry soil as well as if it is excessively wet and the roots are inactive and perhaps decaying.

- Leaves and flowers should be free from blemishes and signs of pests and diseases. Always look under the leaves.

- Don't buy spindly and weak plants – they never recover and later may leave gaps in container displays.

- Don't buy plants exposed to extremes of temperature or strong wind. They may have been chilled or overheated.

COMMON PROBLEMS

Most problems arise from neglect and result from the often large numbers of plants on sale in spring and early summer and the limited time to look after them. Therefore, before buying, remember:

- Where summer-flowering bedding plants are sold in strips or complete trays, check that they are all in a saleable condition. Plants near edges are most vulnerable.

- Where roots of summer-flowering bedding plants only slightly protrude out of the container, it is not a problem; but where they roam further this means breaking them off when removing plants from the container.

- Where roots of container-grown shrubs are matted and protruding out of the container, this indicates neglect and that the plant may have suffered.

RARE PROBLEMS

Garden centers and nurseries have reputations to consider and invariably endeavour to ensure that customers are happy with their plants and will make repeat visits. Presentation as well as quality is all-important to them. Yet this does not apply to all suppliers.

- Dried edges to leaves indicate earlier watering neglect, even though the soil may now be moist.

- Chewed leaves and stems, as well as mottled patches, show that chewing and sucking pests have been present. Look under leaves.

- Wilting stems and leaves may indicate the presence of root-chewing pests as well as the need for water – or even too much water.

WHEN TO BUY

The time of the year to buy plants depends on their nature and uses.

- Spring-flowering bulbs: buy during late summer for planting in early autumn. Available from bulb specialists as well as garden centers and local stores.
- Spring-flowering biennials: buy during late summer for planting in early autumn. Available from garden centers, nurseries and local stores.
- Summer-flowering bedding plants: buy in late spring or early summer and plant as soon as all risk of frost has passed. Available from garden centers, nurseries and local stores.
- Shrubs and trees: container-grown plants can be bought throughout the year and planted whenever the soil and weather are suitable. However, when they are to be grown in containers, planting is best tackled during spring or early summer. Available from garden centers, nurseries and local stores.
- Miniature and slow-growing conifers: invariably sold as container-grown plants throughout the year, but best bought and planted into containers during spring or early summer. Available from garden centers, nurseries and local stores.

GETTING THEM HOME

Getting plants home safely is an early stage in successful container gardening. Here are a few clues to success.

- Ensure there is adequate space in your car for the plants you buy.
- Don't have young children with you.
- Don't have a dog in the car.
- Don't drive fast over pot holes and speed ramps.
- Don't expose plants to drafts.
- Don't leave plants in strong sunlight.

PREPARING CONTAINERS

Getting display containers ready for planting is just as important as preparing plants. Some containers, such as trough-like shells used inside many ornate window boxes, are plain and functional. Others are ornamental and need to be given pre-planting treatment, especially to ensure that they are clean.

Hanging baskets

← Wash and scrub both wire-framed and plastic types to remove dirt and compost that remains from the previous year. Where there is a drip-tray or self-watering device, ensure it is secure and not blocked. Check supporting chains and fixings, as well as screw-type hooks used to suspend the basket.

Window boxes

← Scrub and clean inner boxes as well as ornate outer ones. Check that drainage holes are free and, if using a new, plastic inner box, remove the drainage plugs. Check that wall brackets are secure – eventually they become loose and need tightening or replacing. Never risk them breaking during summer, especially if the display is secured outside an upstairs room.

Troughs

← Scrub and clean troughs. If formed of reconstituted stone, do not use detergents; instead, use warm water and a soft brush. If the trough is large and in a permanent position, plants close by may have encroached on it; cut them back or remove entirely. Check that drainage holes are free.

Pots, urns and tubs

← These are varied in shape as well as materials, which range from plastic and fiberglass to reconstituted stone. Inspect their structure, as well as the positions in which they will eventually be displayed. If made of reconstituted stone and cemented to a plinth, check that is it secure.

Wooden containers

These have varied shapes, from tubs to Versailles planters. Whatever their size and shape, the wood eventually decays and falls apart, especially if constructed of unseasoned, inferior wood. Sometimes removal and disposal is the only solution. Life expectancy can be extended by repairs, but the best preventative measure is to ensure excess water can drain from the base. Also, standing a tub on 3–4 bricks ensures that water drains freely.

PRE-PLANTING TREATMENT

The treatment that should be given to plants either when you get them home or when they arrive by mail order depends on their type.

- Spring-flowering bulbs: unpack them (without mixing up the varieties) and remove any plastic covering. Place the bulbs in a cool, dark, vermin-proof drawer or shed.
- Spring-flowering biennials: these are usually sold as bare-rooted plants in bunches; sometimes the roots are wrapped. Leave them in bunches (to avoid mixing the varieties) and stand these in clean water. Make sure that the roots do not become dry.
- Summer-flowering bedding plants: leave in their containers and stand them outdoors on raised benches to prevent slugs and snails getting at them. Water the plants thoroughly; leaves should be dry by evening.
- Shrubs and trees: if they have been container-grown, the plants should be placed outdoors on a firm surface and watered several times.
- Miniature and slow-growing conifers: these are invariably sold growing in containers; stand them outdoors on a firm surface and water several times.

Window boxes

How can I have color all year?

Window boxes are ideal for creating color throughout the year. Three distinct arrangements of plants – spring, summer, and winter – in three separate inner boxes are needed, and by rotating them in an outer window box it is possible to produce uninterrupted color from one season to another. Some window boxes are just planted with summer-flowering displays, but this is not adventurous and does not use a window box to its full potential.

A window box planted with colorful trailing plants such as Petunias can make a striking display in the summer months in an otherwise dull space.

WHAT ARE THE ADVANTAGES OF USING WINDOW BOXES?

Window boxes introduce many design qualities to patio gardens – as well as front gardens.
- Color can be provided throughout the year by means of three separate and distinctive displays.
- Displays, although they are mainly appreciated from the outside, can also be seen from indoors and through the relevant windows.
- Fragrant flowers can be positioned near windows, where a wide range of scents can waft indoors.
- Where double window box displays are used – with one box positioned about 9 in (23 cm) above the other – the area of wall clothed in color is doubled. Remember to check, however, that the lower box can be reached for watering.
- Window boxes help to unify hanging baskets when positioned on both sides of a window. Color contrasts as well as harmonies are possible between the window box and the hanging baskets, both to suit each other and to contrast with the background.

SELECTING A WINDOW BOX

Choose a window box that harmonizes with the house. Formal types are needed for clinically designed modern houses, while informal ones are better suited to older houses. The range of materials is wide, and includes wood, plastic, fiberglass, terracotta and reconstituted stone, while the design choice is plain or ornate.

Wooden window boxes

Cedar

Painted pine

Pine log effect

Lattice front

Other types of window boxes

Decorated wood

White-painted steel

Terracotta

Reconstituted stone

Plastic lead effect

Plastic kit

Metal frame

Woven willow

MAKING YOUR OWN WINDOW BOX

Wooden window boxes are easy to construct at home. One formed of ¾ in (18 mm) thick wood, and with internal measurements of 32 in (82 cm) long and 8 in (20 cm) deep and wide, is large enough to accommodate an inner box.

Join the boards with galvanized screws

Use strong, straight lumber

Secure strengthening pieces to the base

Drill drainage holes in the base

PHILOSOPHY OF USING WINDOW BOXES

- **In autumn**, plant a spring display and place it outdoors in a sheltered position. In spring, the winter display is removed and the spring display put in its place.
- **In early summer**, replace the spring display with a box that

has been planted with a summer-flowering arrangement.
- **In late summer**, remove the summer display and replace it with the winter display which was previously removed from the window box in early spring.

SPRING
Planted in autumn
Mainly formed of bulbs and spring-flowering hardy biennials

SUMMER
Planted in late spring
Mainly formed of summer-flowering bedding plants

WINTER
Planted in late summer
Mainly formed of hardy foliage plants

POSITIONING WINDOW BOXES

For sash windows, window boxes can be positioned directly on strong sills.

For casement windows, position a window box on brackets and slightly below the sill.

Wall spaces between sash windows benefit from window boxes. Ensure watering is possible.

PLANTING WINDOW BOXES

Plants in window boxes can be either planted directly in compost or left in their pots and plunged (see below right). Summer displays are usually planted into soil in an inner box. Remember to check that water can drain away freely through the drainage holes in the base.

Layer of soil

Layer of peat

Inner, plastic box

Drainage material

Drainage hole in outer container

Broken pieces of clay pots

GOOD WINDOW BOX PLANTS

Window box plants need to be chosen with care. Apart from avoiding plants that are soon buffeted by autumn and winter winds, they must provide reliable displays.

SPRING DISPLAYS:

- Double Daisy – see page 22 • Forget-me-not – see page 22
- Polyanthus – see page 22 • Trumpet Daffodils – see page 39
- Tulips – see page 39 • Wallflower – see page 22

For further plants, see pages 22–23.

SUMMER DISPLAYS:

- Cascade Geraniums – see page 17 • Calceolarias – see page 17
- Fibrous Begonias – see page 16 • Petunias – see page 19
- Tuberous-rooted Begonias – see page 17
- Sweet Alyssum – see page 18

For further plants, see pages 16–20.

WINTER DISPLAYS:

- Small, hardy, evergreen shrubs – see pages 32–33
- Slow-growing and miniature conifers – see pages 34–35
- Trailing evergreen Ivies – see page 23

For further plants, see page 23.

Soils

Whatever the type of soil, it must be clean and free from pests and diseases.

Spring-flowering displays: use well-drained, loam-based soil. This gives plants a firm base that suits spring-flowering bulbs, biennials and, sometimes, a few small conifers and trailing *Hedera helix* (Ivies).

Summer-flowering displays: peat-based soils, with their ability to retain moisture, are ideal for window boxes that need to support a large number of plants.

Winter displays: use well-drained, loam-based soil for these long-term displays, which are mainly formed of miniature slow-growing conifers, trailing ivies and small, evergreen shrubs.

PLUNGING POTS

Instead of removing their pots, some displays – mainly in winter – can be made by plunging pots in moist peat. This method – in contrast to removing pots and planting soil balls directly into compost – enables flowering plants that cease their display or are damaged by frost to be quickly removed and replaced.

Hanging baskets

How should I fill a hanging basket?

When planted, a hanging basket becomes packed with plants that quickly grow and create a magnificent display. The essential needs of these plants are moisture-retentive soil – kept moist throughout summer – and regular feeding to encourage strong and healthy growth. Therefore, careful planting, using clean soil, is essential. Planting a basket is detailed on the opposite page, together with suggestions for suitable soils.

CREATING BEAUTIFUL BASKET DISPLAYS

Use hanging baskets to highlight entrances, but make sure that they cannot be knocked.

Mixing and matching flowering and foliage plants in a hanging basket, as well as color-coordinating them with attractive backgrounds, are ways to get the best out of these popular summer-long features. If planting them yourself is likely to be a time and space problem, established hanging baskets can be bought from nurseries and garden centers in early summer. Sometimes it is possible to choose specific plants and colors if the order is made early, perhaps in mid-winter. To get them home safely, stand large baskets in the top of a round bowl.

Ornate, basket-weave containers have a dainty and rustic appearance.

GUIDE TO SELECTING HANGING BASKETS

Wire-framed hanging baskets range in width from 10–18 in (25 to 45 cm). Choose one with plastic-coated wire. Bowl-shaped plastic hanging baskets have solid sides, which help with moisture retention. Additionally, some of these baskets have drip-trays built into their bases, and these are ideal for displaying plants in porches and conservatories.

Wire round-bottomed hanging basket

Wrought-iron style hanging basket with open sides

Terracotta style ornately decorated hanging basket

Plastic hanging basket with planting pockets and drip-tray

Fit a rounded, plastic container within the basket

DISPLAY POSITIONS

Most hanging baskets are suspended from wall brackets screwed to a wall. This allows the basket to hang freely, with its edge 4–6 in (10–15 cm) from the wall. Screwing large hooks into a bargeboard or fascia is possible for bungalows (but check they are secure).

Suspend a basket from a wall bracket

Hang a basket from a bargeboard or fascia

Secure a basket to an overhead framework

STRONG HARDWARE

Secure fastenings are essential, as well as rust-proof supporting chains. When laden with plants and at the height of summer – and when recently watered – baskets are heavy. Also, wind rocks baskets and loosens weak fixings. Do not hang baskets over sidewalks; excess water drips, and if brackets or chains fail it could be disastrous.

WATERING AND FEEDING TIPS

- Add moisture-retaining additives to the soil (see below).
- Avoid placing baskets in windy positions that will rapidly dry out the soil.
- Place a saucer in the base of the basket (while planting) that will act as a small reservoir.
- If the soil becomes very dry, take down the basket and immerse the soil in water until bubbles cease to rise. Then, allow water to drain before putting it back in position.
- Add slow-acting fertilizers to the soil while planting the basket.
- Regular feeding is essential – first ensure that the soil is moist. Never apply fertilizers while the soil is dry.

Soils

- Specific hanging basket soils are available and some of these have additives that assist in moisture retention.

- Peat-based soils are better than loam-based types for hanging baskets, although they are more difficult to remoisten if they have been allowed to become dry.

- A mixture of equal parts peat-based and loam-based soil is a good compromise; the peat retains moisture and the loam provides food over a longer period.

MOISTURE RETENTION

As an aid to moisture retention in soil, you can add perlite and vermiculite. Earlier, shredded cork was used. Proprietary basket liners (put in place while planting a basket) assist in water retention.

MAKING A BASKET

For an imaginative and attractive basket, create a lattice-work of 9 in (23 cm) long pieces of 1½ in (36 mm) wide and 1 in (25 mm) thick wood by drilling holes in the ends and bolting them together, as shown here. Line the finished basket with sphagnum moss to contain the soil.

SPHAGNUM MOSS OR PLASTIC?

Sphagnum moss is a traditional material for lining wire-framed hanging baskets. It retains moisture in the soil and prevents it falling out. It is also very attractive. Sphagnum moss is difficult to obtain and in its place hanging baskets are usually lined with black plastic.

PLANTING A BASKET

Plants used in hanging baskets are easily damaged by frost. Therefore, if planting is tackled before all risk of frost has passed, ensure there is somewhere the basket can be placed, such as a frost-proof greenhouse. If left outside, plants can be given slight protection by pushing a few sheets of newspaper between the plants and supporting chains.

1 *Place a wire-framed basket in the top of a bucket and line it with black plastic. Mold it to the shape of the basket and cut it off 2 in (5 cm) above the rim. When planting is complete, further trimming is necessary.*

2 *Put a handful of moist peat in the base of the basket, then add soil (see left) to about half the depth of the basket. Gently firm the soil, but take care not to push your fingers through the plastic sheeting.*

3 *Use a sharp knife to make 2 in (5 cm) long slits in the plastic, level with the surface of the soil and about 4 in (10 cm) apart. Push the roots of trailing plants through each hole and cover and firm them with soil.*

4 *Add more soil and plant a dominant, cascading plant in the center, with the top of its rootball about 1 in (2.5 cm) below the basket's rim. Add further plants around it, with trailing types at the edges. Firm the soil.*

5 *When planting is complete, add a thin layer of sphagnum moss (if available) to the surface. This conserves moisture and creates an attractive surface. Leave the basket in the bucket and gently but thoroughly water the soil.*

AFTER-PLANTING CHECKS ...

- Before putting a basket in its display position, inspect it for pests and diseases. Spray if pests such as aphids are seen – they soon multiply and spread if spraying is neglected.
- If you don't think that you will be able to give regular attention to pest control, insert a few insecticide pins into the soil. Plants absorb the chemicals, which kill sucking and chewing insects.
- If giving regular feeds is going to be a problem, insert slow-release fertilizer sticks into the soil.

Baskets in vestibules and porches

Are houseplants hardy enough for a porch?

Inside porches and vestibules only relatively hardy houseplants are likely to be successful in hanging baskets, although much depends on whether the area is open to the elements or enclosed by an outer door. Nevertheless, many indoor plants can normally be grown here, and these are described on pages 44–45. Drip-trays are essential parts of indoor hanging baskets, and plants can either be planted into soil or stood in a flat-based basket (see right).

VESTIBULE AND PORCH DISPLAYS

The choice of positions for hanging baskets to be displayed in vestibules and porches depends on their size and, especially, their width.

• Wherever possible, position a hanging basket away from a door that would direct cold air on plants. However, foliage plants are hardier than most flowering types and, if essential, can be put in a more exposed and cool position.

• Grouping several different plants in the same container creates displays over long periods and several medleys are featured on page 45.

• Narrow vestibules and porches are often able to fit in small, wall-fixed baskets rather than ones suspended from a bracket. Many suitable plants are described on pages 44–45.

GETTING THE DISPLAY RIGHT

When planting an outdoor hanging basket, most plants are small and perhaps removed from "strips" of plants or bought separately but without an attractive pot. Conversely, plants used in hanging baskets in vestibules and porches invariably are established in pots. For this reason, it is easier to plan a display in detail before transferring the design and plants to a basket.

• Draw a circle on a piece of paper to the same size and shape of the basket.

• Place a dominant plant in the center of the circle and cluster others around it, in varying positions until an attractive display is created.

• It is an ideal way to use available plants to the best advantage.

• When the design is complete, transfer them to the hanging basket.

Hanging baskets introduce added color and vitality to a porch, but make sure they cannot be knocked or prevent doors opening.

... don't get the floor wet

Drip-trays that are integrated into the structure are essential parts of hanging baskets to be used in vestibules and porches. There are several excellent designs on the market.

PORCH AND VESTIBULE OPTIONS

Porches and vestibules offer attractive homes for plants in hanging baskets that have integral drip-trays (see page 54). These areas are usually unheated and porches are often colder and more exposed than vestibules.

In a porch

↗ *During summer, both outdoor hanging basket plants and hardy houseplants can be used, but in winter hardy foliage plants are better at surviving low temperatures.*

In a vestibule

↗ *Medleys of flowering and attractively foliaged houseplants are ideal for vestibules, especially during summer. In winter, give more prominence to those that have attractive foliage.*

PLANTING OPTIONS

There are two options when planting a hanging basket for a porch or vestibule. One is to plant directly into soil; the other is to leave plants in their pots. With both methods, thoroughly water the plants the day before planting. Here are details of tackling both of these methods.

Planting into soil

Step 4
Pack and firm soil between plants, as well as slightly over them. Gently but thoroughly water the plants and soil.

Step 3
Remove the pots and position plants on top of the soil, with their tops ½–¾ in (12–18 mm) below the rim.

Step 2
Spread peat-based potting soil over the pea gravel until about 6 in (15 cm) below the rim of the basket.

Step 1
Thoroughly clean and dry the basket. Then, spread a ¾–1 in (18–25 mm) thick layer of pea gravel over the base.

Leaving pots in place

Step 3
Check that the plants are positioned, as earlier designed (see left), and pack moist peat between the pots.

Step 2
Place the pots and plants in position. Ensure that the tops of the pots are about 1 in (2.5 cm) below the rim.

Step 4
Do not cover compost. Plants are watered individually and therefore it is essential that the soil can be seen.

Step 1
Select a plastic, flat-bottomed, indoor hanging basket and spread a 1 in (2.5 cm) thick layer of pea gravel over the base.

WATERING AND FEEDING

Like all other plants in containers, plants in hanging baskets need regular watering, especially during summer.
• In hanging baskets where plants are left in their pots it is necessary to check each plant individually to see if the soil is becoming dry. Remember that large plants in small pots need more frequent watering than small plants in large pots. Ensure that plants are not given too much water.
• Where pots have been removed and plants are growing in the same soil, keep the soil evenly moist, but not excessively wet.

Soils

• When planting: where pots are removed, so that plants can be planted into soil, use a peat-based type. To assist in moisture-retention, add some clay granules to the soil.

• Leaving pots in place: where each plant is left in its pot, use moist peat to pack around and between the pots to keep their soil moist and cool, especially when they are to be hung in a warm atmosphere.

HARDWARE

Use strong hardware. Sometimes, cup-hooks can be screwed into beams in the ceilings of porches and vestibules. Take care, especially in constricted areas, that wall-secured brackets cannot injure eyes. A range of hardware is shown on page 54. Plastic-coated and ornate metal types are available.

FOCAL DISPLAYS

In large vestibules, out-of-the-way corners can be brightened by using groups of plants – some standing on the floor and others in hanging baskets. Use a combination of plants – mix variegated foliage types and others with flowers. Additionally, use a spotlight to highlight the feature and turn it into a focal point.

REPLACING PLANTS

Where plants are left in their pots, plants can be replaced when they stop being attractive. Take care when doing this not to damage neighboring plants. Before putting a new plant into position, first water the soil and allow excess moisture to drain.

SMARTENING UP PLANTS

Eventually, hanging baskets where plants are collectively grown in the same soil need to be smartened up, especially when vigorous plants dominate their neighbors. Sometimes, shoots and branches can be snipped off, but usually it is best to start again. Some plants can be reused, whereas others need to be replaced.

Baskets

Are baskets a good choice?

Wall baskets and free-standing baskets are increasingly popular and available in a range of sizes and materials. Free-standing baskets are sold in widths from 12–28 in (30 to 72 cm), with increases of about 4 in (10 cm). Wire-framed wall baskets range in width from 9–20 in (23 to 50 cm). Plastic and terracotta types are usually more decorative and available in widths from 6–10 in (15 to 25 cm). These are ideal for positioning alongside a small, narrow entrance.

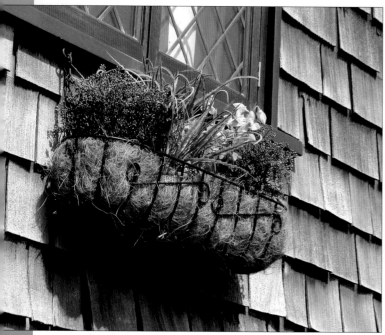

Ornate wire-framed wall baskets can be suspended from a stout sill where wall coverings such as shingles prevent the drilling of holes. Ensure that all hardware is firmly attached.

Bland and unappealing walls can be given vitality and eye appeal by securing wall baskets to them. Throughout the summer months, they can be drenched with color.

DECORATING WALLS

Wall baskets can be used to create magnificent displays. They are mainly positioned at waist height and can be displayed in many different places.

- Wide free-standing baskets can be used under windows, instead of window boxes. With their rustic appearance they harmonize well with old properties.
- Position small wall baskets between windows and, perhaps, in combination with a window box or free-standing basket underneath a window.
- Small wall baskets are ideal for positioning on walls at the sides of doors.
- Placed at waist height along a wall, they can introduce extra color to an otherwise bland area.
- They excel when positioned along the fronts of row houses, where paving abuts the property. Unlike floor-positioned containers, such as tubs and troughs, they enable the area underneath them to be hosed and cleaned without any difficulty.
- Plastic and terracotta wall baskets are ideal for balcony walls, but take care that water cannot mark the wall.

WALL-BASKET OPTIONS

Simple wire basket

Wrought-iron style basket

Aluminum non-rusting basket

Ornate wire basket

Corner basket

Miniature baskets

FREE-STANDING BASKET OPTIONS

Simple wire

Ornate

Miniature

PLANTING A WALL BASKET

When planting a wall basket, ensure that excess water cannot run out of the back of the container and trickle down a wall.

1 *Hold a wall basket in place and mark the positions of the securing holes. Drill, insert wall anchors and screw the container on to the wall.*

2 *Line the inside with strong, black plastic (or two layers of bin-liners). Ensure the back is covered to prevent water getting on the wall and staining it.*

3 *Fill the basket to about half full with soil. Then use a pointed knife to pierce holes in the plastic, but only at the front.*

4 *Start planting the basket from the back, putting in some bushy plants that will give height to the display. Firm soil around and over them.*

5 *Add further plants, with trailing types positioned along the front edge. Add and firm further soil until ¾ in (18 mm) below the rim. Gently water the plants.*

GOOD PLANTS FOR BASKETS

Many plants can be used in these types of containers, for both spring- and summer-flowering displays. Here are a few clues that will guide you to success.

Spring displays:
- When using Tulips, select short-stemmed types that will not be at risk from blustery, late winter and spring weather.
- *Muscari armeniacum* (Grape Hyacinths) are more tolerant of wind, as are the variegated small-leaved *Hedera helix* (Ivies) so often used in spring displays.

Summer displays:
- Always ensure that the soil is covered with leaves and flowers; bare soil in baskets is always unappealing.
- Preferably, use dome-shaped and bushy plants, with trailing types at the edges to cloak the container.
- Unlike hanging baskets, which are admired at shoulder or head height, wall baskets are positioned at waist level and therefore are admired from above. Bright-faced, upward-facing flowers are therefore desirable.

Soils

- Use peat-based soil in wall baskets, especially for summer displays; but for spring displays planted in early autumn it is better to use well-drained, loam-based soil.

- In large mangers, a mixture of equal parts loam-based and peat-based soil gives good results, especially if the soil is left in the container for a couple of years.

- For a small wall basket, add moisture-retaining materials to the soil.

WATERING AND FEEDING

- Regular watering and feeding is essential throughout summer. While doing this, however, take care not to stand too close to the display as water may drip from drainage slits made in the container's front.
- During winter, less watering is needed. However, in late winter and early spring regularly check that the soil is lightly moist.

AFTERCARE

- In late spring, remove all plants after they cease flowering. Discard biennials, but bulbous types can be planted around other plants such as shrubs in mixed borders.
- In late summer or early autumn, remove summer-flowering displays. Add further soil (as needed) or completely refurbish the basket, and plant a spring-flowering display.

DISPLAY COMBINATIONS

Using color-themed baskets against color harmonizing and contrasting walls is described on pages 12–13. Here are a couple of combinations of plants to consider, for spring and summer displays.

Spring displays

← These do not have to be packed with rare and expensive plants. Here is a medley of bright-faced Pansies, variegated small-leaved *Hedera helix* (Ivies) and the variegated *Lamium maculatum* 'Album,' with mid-green leaves that reveal a central silver stripe.

Summer displays

← For a dramatic two-plant display, use a dominant planting of a red Verbena, with the addition of variegated small-leaved *Hedera helix* (Ivies). This is best seen against a white background, although it will also look good on a red-brick wall.

Stone, glazed and hypertufa sinks

Do I need a special sink?

Old, shallow, stone sinks are ideal containers for alpine and small rock-garden plants. Miniature and slow-growing conifers are also candidates, as well as miniature bulbs. Deeper, glazed sinks can also be used, but they benefit from being modified and given an aged, rustic appearance (see below). Sinks made of reconstituted stone have a natural appearance, and while some have a traditional sink shape others have a quarter-circle shape.

MODIFYING A DEEP, GLAZED SINK

Small border plants and culinary herbs can also be used in stone sinks.

- Wash the sink with soap and water and stand it on four bricks that are positioned slightly in from the edges.
- Use an old chisel to scratch the outside and to about 3 in (7.5 cm) down the inside edge. Wash and allow surfaces to dry.
- Paint scratched surfaces with a PVA bonding glue.
- Mix 1 part coarse sand, 1 part cement powder and 2 parts fine peat (all parts by bulk). Add water and mix to a stiff paste. Before the PVA glue hardens, wear gloves and coat all scratched surfaces with this mixture. Press it firmly against the sides.
- Leave the sink in a dry, cool, frost-proof shed for a few weeks.

PREPARING STONE SINKS

Always handle stone sinks with care. They appear strong, but if twisted awkwardly on one edge and knocked can soon crack. Use soapy water to clean the sink, inside and out, and thoroughly rinse with clean water. Until needed for planting, stand it on bricks.

Another type of container to modify

Used fiberglass shower bases, which are usually about 28 in (72 cm) square and 6 in (15 cm) deep, can be coated in the same way as a deep, glazed sink (see left). However, the shell lacks rigidity and needs to be put in its final position before it is modified.

PLANTING SCHEMES FOR STONE SINKS

PLANTING SCHEME

Campanula cochlearifolia
Antennaria dioica
Edraianthus pumilio
Erinus alpinus
Lewisia cotyledon
Hebe buchananii

This display drenches the sink in a wide range of colors throughout the spring and summer months.

PLANTING SCHEME

Miniature conifer
Saxifraga cotyledon
Sedum spathulifolium
Sempervivum tectorum
Armeria maritima
Arabis alpina

The addition of a miniature conifer introduces height as well as color to this attractive planting scheme.

PLANTING A STONE SINK

Place a clean stone sink in position, on four stout bricks and with a slight slope to the drainage hole. A warm, sheltered position in good light and away from over-hanging deciduous trees is essential; fallen leaves on top of plants encourage decay.

1 *Crumple a piece of wire-netting and press it firmly into the drainage hole. Then, over the top place a large piece of broken clay pot to prevent soil blocking the hole.*

2 *Cover the base with a 1 in (2.5 cm) thick layer of pea gravel. Then, spread a 1½–2 in (36–50 mm) thick layer of granulated peat over the pea gravel.*

3 *On a large piece of paper, mark the shape of the sink. Place it on the ground and spread out the plants to be planted into the container in an attractive manner.*

4 *Fill and firm the sink with soil to within 1 in (2.5 cm) of the rim; use a trowel to do the planting. Firm the soil and spread stone chippings over the top.*

SOIL FOR SINK GARDENS

A well-drained, loam-based soil combined with extra coarse sand and peat is suitable for most plants in a sink garden. For lime-hating plants, omit the chalk in the soil or buy a special proprietary mixture for acid-loving plants.

WATERING AND FEEDING TIPS

- From mid-spring to autumn, regularly water the soil, taking care not to excessively splash water on soft, hairy leaves. Do not disturb the pea gravel, as this helps to keep the soil cool and moist during summer, and prevent heavy rain splashing soil on plants.
- Feeding is not usually necessary as over-lush and rampant plants are not attractive in sinks. However, plants that have been in a sink for several years benefit from a low-nitrogen, granular fertilizer applied in spring and once more in mid-summer. Keep the fertilizer off leaves.

HOW TO MAKE A HYPERTUFA SINK

A hypertufa sink is an exciting feature and not difficult to make. It has a natural, tufa-like appearance and is ideal for alpine plants.

1 Its construction means using a bare piece of firm, level, somewhat clay soil as a mold. Using strings, mark a rectangle 2 ft (60 cm) long and 16 in (40 cm) wide.
2 With a builder's trowel, carefully remove soil from the area to about 2 in (5 cm) deep, leaving the sides square and intact.
3 Mark an area 3 in (7.5 cm) wide around the original rectangle and, using a trowel, excavate this to 7 in (18 cm) deep. This creates the mold for the sides.
4 Carefully hammer two dowels – about 1 in (2.5 cm) thick – into the base. Later, these will be the drainage holes.
5 Prepare hypertufa: by parts, mix 1 of cement powder, 1 of coarse sand and 4 of clean, moderately dry, granulated peat. Add water to form a stiff but pliable paste.
6 Fill and firm the sides, as well as 1 in (2.5 cm) in depth on the top, with the mixture.
7 Place galvanized netting over the top and then a further 1 in (2.5 cm) of the mixture. Smooth with a builder's trowel or float. Cover the sink with a protective covering and allow it to set for at least a couple of weeks.
8 Carefully dig out the sink, ease out the stakes, wash it and place it in its display position. Stand the sink on firm supports such as strong bricks (see above right).

↗ *Hypertufa sinks have an attractive, informal and rustic appearance.*

↗ *Stand the sink on strong bricks to make plants easier to see, but do not block the drainage holes.*

↗ *During construction (see step 4, left), hammer two dowels into the base to create the drainage holes.*

Troughs and planters

What are troughs?

Planters and troughs are versatile containers and range from simple yet effective plastic ones to large and ornate types formed of reconstituted stone. Others are made of wood, terracotta or fiberglass. In size they also vary, from 20 in (50 cm) long troughs, that can be placed on walls and floors of balconies and create homes for ephemeral plants, to large and dominant types that provide growing places for more permanent plants, including small shrubs.

SELECTING A TROUGH OR PLANTER

Ornate oval planter

Reconstituted stone trough

Gothic style resin planter

Wooden trough incorporating a trellis

The practical qualities required of a trough are that it is well drained, creates a secure base for plants and holds enough soil to provide food and moisture for plants. Additionally, there are aesthetic factors, such as ensuring that the trough harmonizes with its position in a garden. There are many different designs, both clinical and ornate.

Planting summer-flowering plants

As soon as the risk of frost has passed in late spring or early summer, summer-flowering plants can be planted. Place broken pieces of clay pot over drainage holes, then a layer of pea gravel. Add soil and set the plants in position. Firm the soil and gently but thoroughly water the soil.

Moisture-retentive soil

Well-drained base

TROUGHS ON LEGS

As well as placing troughs at patio level, or at the sides of balconies, they look good when raised up on legs. Here are some ideas to try.

- Ornate, wrought-iron designs are available from garden centers and mail-order catalogs and usually display troughs at about 2 ft (60 cm) high. Because the supporting framework is attractive, the trough can be plain so that it will not compete for attention.
- Rustic wooden troughs can be placed on stout wooden legs, again with an informal shape.
- Reconstituted stone troughs are perfectly complemented by ornate plinths in a similar material. Ensure that they are load-bearing and will support the trough when filled with plants and moist soil.

SOILS FOR TROUGHS

- Summer-flowering displays: peat-based soils are ideal. They provide a moisture-retentive medium and some fertilizers. However, you will need to feed plants throughout summer.

- Spring displays: use loam-based soil for bulbs and spring-flowering biennials.

- Perennial displays: use well-drained loam-based soil for long-term flowers. Add extra coarse sand to the mixture.

USING TROUGHS

Troughs are versatile and can be used in many different positions in a garden, as well as on balconies. However, wherever they are positioned, ensure that water can drain freely from the trough yet not inconvenience people. Here are a few places to consider.

↗ *Brighten up any dull floor areas that are close to walls.*

↗ *At the edges of balconies, allow plants to trail through the bars.*

↗ *Liven up uninteresting courtyard walls with a wall-secured trough.*

Raised beds

Raised beds are permanent features in gardens, constructed usually of bricks but occasionally stout wooden boards. They are often an integral part of a patio or terrace and sometimes have built-in sitting and relaxing positions as part of their design. Raised beds enable plants to be displayed throughout the year and are especially useful where the soil is not suitable for the plants you want to grow – too chalky or too acid, or even if badly drained.

What are raised beds?

CHOICE OF RAISED BEDS

Reconstituted stone blocks   *Rustic log-rolls*   *Brick bed with capping*   *Low brick wall*

Raised beds must be strongly constructed and harmonize with the nature of the garden. Log-rolls and reconstituted stone exude informality, while brick-edged beds have a formal appearance. Well-drained soil is essential, and a mixture of clean, weed-free topsoil and coarse sand is suitable. Ensure that water in soil in a raised bed can easily drain away; the build-up of water in soil can eventually cause the sides of the raised bed to collapse.

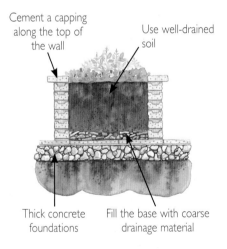

Mediterranean-style feature with raised beds. Colored gravel creates extra interest.

AN L-SHAPED RAISED BED

➔ Tall, raised beds are ideal for gardeners in wheelchairs or for those who are unable to bend down easily. Ensure that the brickwork is safe and that the bricks are well bonded together. Leave some weeping holes in the sides for the free drainage of water from the soil.

A capping along the wall's top is essential to ensure that rainwater does not enter the bricks and vertical bonds, thus weakening the structure.

By constructing an L-shaped raised bed, a much stronger feature will be created than would be the case with a long and narrow type.

Strong foundations are essential to ensure a long life for the raised bed. Wide foundations are better than narrow ones for each wall.

STONE RAISED BED

Cement a capping along the top of the wall

Use well-drained soil

Thick concrete foundations

Fill the base with coarse drainage material

Permanent raised beds are ideal for constructing on an existing patio that has a strong, thick base. Such beds can be built of bricks, reconstituted stone or concrete blocks, and may be positioned exactly to your preferred design. For ease of construction, a square or rectangular shape is always best, and this should be built to a height not exceeding 2½ ft (75 cm). Remember to leave small weeping holes between the lower parts of the brickwork to enable any excess water to escape freely.

Pots, tubs and urns

Pots, tubs and urns are popular features on patios and terraces, as they can be grouped to create varied displays that suit the shape and background of the area. A couple of dominant urns at the top or bottom of a flight of steps can also be dramatic. If planted with light-colored foliage or bright flowers, they help to define the edges of the steps during late-summer evenings. Herb planters are ideal for displays in cottage and informal gardens.

PLANTING A SHRUB IN A TUB

Well-drained loam-based soil

Strong, healthy shrub

Thick layer of pebbles

Layer of moist peat

Drainage holes in the base

Shrubs and small trees are long-term plants in tubs and therefore need careful planting.

1 Select a large, strong tub with drainage holes drilled in its base. Stand the tub on three strong bricks.
2 Form a layer of large pebbles in the base to ensure the drainage holes do not become blocked. Add a 2 in (5 cm) layer of moist peat.
3 Add loam-based soil and firm it to form a slight mound.
4 Remove the container from the shrub (watered during the previous day) and position it on the mound. The top of the soil ball should be about 1½ in (36 mm) below the tub's rim.
5 Add further soil and firm it around the soil ball. The soil, when potting is complete, should be 1 in (2.5 cm) below the rim.
6 Lightly but thoroughly water the soil to settle it around the roots.

POT, TUB AND URN OPTIONS

↘ *The range of attractive containers for plants is impressively wide.*

Large plastic pot

Terracotta "long Toms"

Flared-shape terracotta pot

Decorated glazed pot

Glazed ceramic pot

Glazed ceramic pot

Stone-effect pot

Terracotta pot

Strawberry or herb planter

Half-barrel

Decorative lead-effect tub

Large handmade terracotta urns

Victorian architectural "vase" on a plinth

Wall pot

Wall bracket for three pots

Wall bracket for one pot

Decorative pot

Modern aluminum pot

PLANTING A HERB PLANTER

Plant herbs in the top as well as the sides

Thick layer of pebbles

Loam-based soil

Wire-netting tube filled with pebbles

Herbs remain in planters for several years, until they outgrow the container.

1 Place a clean planter in its display position. Stand it on three bricks so that drainage holes are not blocked.

2 Form a layer of large pebbles in the base. Then, roll a piece of wire-netting to form a 3 in (7.5 cm) wide tube. Stand it in the center of the planter and with its base on the pebbles. Fill it with pebbles. Fill the base of the planter with loam-based soil to the level of the lowest planting hole.

3 Push the roots of a herb through the hole and on to the soil. Add and firm soil around them; then add further soil. In turn, put a herb in each hole and firm soil around its roots.

PLANTING DAFFODILS IN A SINGLE LAYER

Position bulbs about 1½ in (36 mm) apart

Thick layer of coarse drainage material

Large, golden-faced, Trumpet Daffodils create magnificent displays in spring. To achieve this, bulbs need to be planted in early autumn.

1 Thoroughly clean a large tub and check that drainage holes are not blocked. Position the tub on 3–4 bricks and in its display position.

2 Add a 2 in (5 cm) layer of coarse drainage material to the base, then firm loam-based soil until 8 in (20 cm) below the tub's top.

3 Space out healthy bulbs on the soil, leaving about 1½ in (36 mm) between them. Then add further soil – without disturbing the bulbs – until 1 in (2.5 cm) below the tub's rim. Gently but thoroughly water the soil.

PLANTING DAFFODILS IN A DOUBLE LAYER

When Daffodil bulbs are planted in two layers, an even more dramatic and colorful display is created.

1 Prepare a tub in the same way as for a single layer (see left).

2 Add and firm soil to 8 in (20 cm) below the tub's top. Space out the bulbs, about 3 in (7.5 cm) apart, on top of the soil.

3 Trickle and firm soil over them to just below their necks. Then, position a further row of bulbs between them.

4 Add and firm further soil to within 1 in (2.5 cm) of the top. Gently but thoroughly water the soil.

Position bulbs in two layers

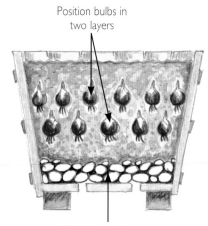

Thick layer of coarse drainage material

HOW TO MAKE A WOODEN PLANTER

↘ → A low, wooden planter is easy and quick to construct – and if second-hand lumber is available it will also be inexpensive. Don't make it more than 12–15 in (30–38 cm) high, as it will then lose rigidity. Indeed, a strong base is essential to give it structural support and a long life.

Step 4
Screw a framework of wood to the upper edge to form a cap.

Step 3
Construct a framework of wood to the same size as the base. Nail or screw this to the tops of the side planks.

Step 1
Cut strong planks to form a base. Nail or screw the planks to a framework of side and end lumber that will give the base extra rigidity and form supports for the sides.

Step 2
Cut the side planks to length and then nail or screw them to the base. Ensure that they fit closely together.

Container water features

How can I create a miniature water garden?

Few features on patios create as much interest as miniature water gardens in tubs and deep stone sinks. Metal casks are sometimes used, but the temperature of water in them fluctuates throughout summer and takes a dive in autumn. Wooden tubs are the best containers as the water's temperature is then more stable. Be prepared to remove fish in autumn. Including a small fountain to keep water moving diminishes the likelihood of creating a mosquito breeding ground.

USING A TUB

Select a large, deep, clean tub and place it in its display position. Fill the tub with water and check for any leaks. If it is not watertight, line it with black plastic (cut off level with the top). Fill with clean water. Put in water plants in late spring or early summer. Plant them in individual plastic-mesh containers; with Waterlilies, stand the pot on a few bricks so that the pads float. As the plants grow, gradually remove the bricks. Regularly check that the water level is up to the rim. In summer, water soon evaporates and the level drops.

Stand marginal plants on inverted pots

Regularly top up the pool with water throughout summer

Stand Waterlilies on bricks so that their pads float

↗ *Half-barrels are easily converted into miniature water features for display on a patio, but they must be watertight.*

USING A STONE SINK

Water features in stone sinks soon capture attention, but because of the shallowness of the container only small Waterlilies and other plants are practical (see right). Also, because the water's temperature plummets in a stone sink (although less than in a metal container), it is usually necessary to remove all fish (if present) and plants in autumn and to place them in a cold greenhouse. Rapid temperature fluctuations soon distress fish.

More container ideas

Stone sinks or troughs create superb water features

Concrete dishes are ideal for displays of water plants

Galvanized metal containers make distinctive features

FOLIAGE DISPLAYS IN SMALL CONTAINERS

Small containers – some of metal and others terracotta – can be used for summer displays of miniature water plants. If the container is small, put only one plant in it, rather than a collection. In autumn, move the plants and containers to a cold greenhouse, where they will be safe from frost.

Small containers hold insufficient water for fish, but they are ideal for creating displays of water plants.

Barrels

Select a barrel with care, and use only genuine half-barrels with metal hoops and shaped staves – rather than one of the badly made and inferior imitations that are available.

Look for a genuine oak half-barrel with iron hoops. Drive in screws just below the hoops, to hold them in place. Soak the barrel in water until the wood swells within the hoops, making the barrel watertight.

Oak staves angled so that they fit together

Iron hoops; screw them in place to prevent them slipping

SOIL FOR WATER PLANTS

The best soil for water plants is a heavy loam that has been enriched with a sprinkling of bonemeal to encourage rapid root development. Ensure that the loam is free from decaying debris, such as old roots. After planting, add a layer of clean pea gravel on the top of the container to prevent the soil being disturbed and clouding the water.

WATER-GARDEN PLANTS FOR TUBS AND SINKS

The key to success with Waterlilies and other water plants in small containers such as tubs, half-barrels and sinks is to select only those that are likely to grow well in a limited amount of space. The Waterlilies suggested below are either dwarf or small varieties that will happily grow in water that is up to 10 in (25 cm) deep. As soon as any water plant starts to dominate its container, lift it out and replace it with a smaller one that is more in proportion.

Miniature Waterlilies

Nymphaea 'Laydekeri Lilacea'

Nymphaea 'Paul Hariot'

Nymphaea 'Sioux'

Nymphaea 'Pygmaea Helvola'

Water plants

Carex elata 'Aurea' (also known as *Carex stricta* 'Bowles' Golden')

Schoenoplectus lacustris tabernaemontani 'Zebrinus' (also known as *Scirpus zebrinus*)

Iris laevigata 'Variegata'

Typha minima

HOW TO BUILD A BUBBLING URN FEATURE

You need a plastic sump for the reservoir, a ceramic pot or urn (shape and size to suit), a small pump, about 10 ft (3 m) of water-delivery pipe, a sheet of wire mesh and a bucket of cobbles.

Step 5
Fill the urn and the sump with water.

Step 4
Cover the mesh and pipes with a display of rocks and stones, so that the pipes are hidden.

Step 3
Cover the sump with wire mesh and set the urn in position on top of it. Run the water-delivery pipe into the urn.

Step 2
Put the pump in the reservoir and protect the cable with a length of water pipe. Connect the water-delivery pipe to the pump.

Step 1
Dig a hole for the sump. Set it in place with sand packed all around it.

HOW TO BUILD A WALL-MASK WATERSPOUT

If you have a patio with a brick wall at one side, you can have a wall-mask waterspout. Use a ready-made trough or tank or build a brick reservoir to match the wall. If drilling holes through the wall is not an option, mount copper water pipe to the face of the wall and conceal it with foliage.

Step 4
Fix the mask to the wall. Install the water pipe that connects the pump to the mask. Fit plastic trunking to protect the water pipe and cable from damage.

Step 5
Fill the reservoir to the brim with clean water. Set the pump flow to suit and switch on.

Step 1
Position a stone trough or a metal tank; alternatively build a brick reservoir.

Step 3
Sit the pump in the reservoir and run the cable and water pipe through the hole. Drill another hole in the wall at the point where you want the mask to go.

Step 2
Drill a hole through the wall, just above the reservoir, big enough to take the water pipe and the pump cable.

Grow bags on patios

Grow bags are versatile and functional containers that create instant homes for flowering and food plants. However, the relatively shallow depth of the soil suits only those plants with fibrous or short roots. Nevertheless, there are many plants to use and places to position them, including near kitchen doors and planted with culinary herbs, on flat roofs and cloaked with trailing flowers, on patios and planted with tomato plants.

How do I use a grow bag?

THRIFTY GARDENING!

Grow bags are not single-use containers. As well as providing homes for many and varied plants – from vegetables and herbs to flowering plants – during one season, they can be reused the following year. Even after that season, the soil can be removed and scattered on beds and borders in order to improve the soil.

PREPARING A GROW BAG

The soil in grow bags when stacked in garden centers becomes compressed. Therefore, before using a grow bag, thorough preparation is needed (see page 47). Additionally, placing the bag on a wooden pallet enables it to be easily moved when planted, as well as making it more difficult for slugs and snails to reach the plants.

↗ *On patios, support is needed for tomato plants*

↗ *Reduce risk from slugs by raising the bag off the ground*

↗ *Many flowering plants are ideal for a grow bag*

Growing tomatoes in growing-bags

Plant three cordon types (single, upright stems) in a standard grow bag. Supports are essential – proprietary metal types are available, but home-made types fashioned from bamboo canes and wires are possible. In a greenhouse, it is possible to push bamboo canes right into the grow bag and into the soil in it. The tops of the canes can be tied to a supporting framework of canes and wires. Pushing canes all the way through a grow bag in this way ensures that any excess moisture is able to escape.

For growing other vegetables in grow bags, see pages 46–47. For detailed information on growing potatoes in grow bags, see right.

MULTI-PLACE CONTAINERS

Few plant containers are as versatile as grow bags. As well as being placed on a patio or terrace and used for vegetables, they are ideal for introducing summer-flowering plants to the tops of flat roofs, either on home extensions or on garages. Put bushy plants in them, as well as trailing types that will cloak the sides.

Watering plants positioned on the tops of roofs is difficult and proprietary fittings for hoses are available. Additionally, a hose when secured by wires to a strong bamboo cane, and with a bent end, enables easy watering.

Growing potatoes in grow bags

Potatoes can be grown in special potato-growing containers, as well as in large pots (see pages 46–47), but they can also be easily cultivated in grow bags on a patio. Follow the instructions given below.

- In early to mid-spring, prepare a grow bag; thoroughly shake the bag in order to loosen the compost. Place the grow bag on a patio or pallet. Do not cut away any of the plastic. If the soil is dry, water it thoroughly through the slits.

- Push one healthy tuber of an early potato variety, so that it is near the base of the grow bag and covered with soil.

- Bury the potato starters several inches deep in the soil.

- Regularly check that the soil is moist. However, do not add too much water.

- Shoots arise from the soil and if there is a risk of frost cover them at night with newspaper.

- When you are ready for an early crop of new potatoes, harvest the tubers.

- There is no need to harvest all of the potatoes at the same time; but cover the tubers with soil, especially if frost is forecast over the next few days.

Planting pockets and shelves

Unusual yet practical features can be built into patios to create extra color. These range from a few bricks, pavers or paving slabs left out of a patio floor to provide ground-level growing spaces, to alcoves and recesses carefully fitted into walls and screens. The sides of garden steps can also be made more exciting, with plants in pots positioned along them. All of these features make a patio unique, more interesting and an extension of your home.

Can I create extra patio color?

Rustic containers, imitating hollowed tree trunks, are novel.

Planting pockets on walls provide opportunities for small plants.

Designer gaps in walls are ideal for small, cascading plants.

Bricks or pavers omitted from patios create spaces for plants.

PLANTING POCKETS

Planting pockets left in a patio's floor are ideal for small, low, creeping plants, including thyme and other cottage-garden plants often planted between natural stone paving. However, take care after snowfalls not to stand on them, nor to clear snow and ice by using a shovel or scattering salt over the area – it soon kills them.

POUCH GARDENING

These are exciting containers for annual patio plants and can be fixed to walls and fences. Basically, they are black plastic tubes which hold soil and into which trailing and bushy plants can be planted. Suitable plants include trailing Lobelias, Pansies, Busy Lizzies, trailing Petunias and Verbenas. You can raise the plants yourself or buy them from garden centers or nurseries. It is also possible to grow culinary herbs in pouches, which is ideal for small gardens.

Alcoves

Small alcoves and recesses are ideal for containers.

Recesses where a garden seat for two can be positioned create romantic opportunities, especially when cloaked with fragrant climbers such as *Lonicera* (Honeysuckle) and *Jasminum officinale* (Common Jasmine). Rustic trellises and pergolas often have arches built into them, while screen-block walling is sufficiently versatile to have plant-cloaked recesses. You could try covering them with *Clematis montana* (Mountain Clematis), which is sufficiently vigorous to drench them in leaves, with pretty flowers being produced during late spring and early summer.

In addition to large alcoves for seats and, perhaps, benches, small ones (see left) are popular for displaying pots and troughs. If the area is shallow, use upright plants that can be highlighted by a rounded arch.

SHELVES FOR CONTAINERS

As well as constructing recesses in walls so that plants can be put in them, consider leaving a brick or tile projecting so that you can place a plant on it. Protruding bricks built into walls alongside garden steps are attractive, but ensure that the flight of steps is sufficiently wide so that arms do not knock against them.

Protruding bricks from walls make perfect ledges for small pot plants.

BENCHES

Benches with soil constrained by bricks or old railroad ties create unusual features; at seat level, sow grass seed or plant Thyme. An alternative is to plant the non-flowering and low-growing form of Chamomile, *Chamaemelum nobile* 'Treneague' (also known as *Anthemis nobilis* 'Treneague'). It needs little trimming and when the foliage is bruised reveals a refreshing Chamomile-like redolence.

Wheelbarrows

Part of the pleasure of container-gardening is creating unusual containers for plants, and few are as captivating as a wheelbarrow. Old wooden wheelbarrows, as well as non-industrial metal types, create superb homes for summer-flowering plants, especially when painted and positioned against a wall in a contrasting or harmonizing color. Drainage holes in the base are essential to ensure that the soil does not become waterlogged.

A wheelbarrow bursting with summer color creates a fine focal point in a garden.

PLANTING A WHEELBARROW

- Check that the wheelbarrow is sound (see below), then put it in its display position.
- To prevent the wood in the base decaying (or the metal rusting), line the whole area with a layer of plastic. Puncture it to create drainage holes, matching the positions of those in the wooden or metal base.
- Add a thick layer of pebbles to ensure excess water escapes from the soil.
- Fill and firm the wheelbarrow with well-drained, loam-based soil. If the wheelbarrow is large, add extra coarse sand.
- Start planting in the middle of the wheelbarrow, using dominant plants; work outwards until trailing types are positioned around the outside.
- Trim the plastic level with the top when planting is complete.
- Gently but thoroughly water the plants. If there is still a risk of frost, cover the plants with newspaper at night to protect them.

MAKING A MINIATURE WOODEN WHEELBARROW

Rather than making a full-sized wooden wheelbarrow, it is much easier to construct a miniature one about 12 in (30 cm) high, 11 in (27 cm) wide and 35 in (89 cm) long. For this, you will require the following items:

- five sides to form a box (plus 26 galvanized screws);
- two legs (plus 2 galvanized screws for each);
- two handles (in marine plywood), with bolt-size holes in the wheel-end;
- one wheel (made of thick, marine plywood), with a large central hole, drilled and with two washers;
- one bolt (for fixing the wheel).

Adding gnomes

To complete this diminutive and unusual feature, position a few statues of gnomes all around the miniature wheelbarrow. Choose statues that have accompanying containers, in which you can grow flowering plants.

Step 4
Screw the sides of the box to the base.

Step 3
Screw the base of the box to the handles, leaving room for the wheel to turn.

Step 1
Screw the handles to the legs.

Step 2
Position the wheel and, using the bolt and washers, secure it between the handles, which also form the main supporting framework.

CHECKING A WHEELBARROW

Always check wheelbarrows thoroughly in spring before they are filled with soil and put in their display positions.

- Inspect wheel brackets as well as leg and handle fixings. For wooden wheelbarrows, metal brackets can be screwed into place, while for metal types tightening up bolts is usually all that is needed.
- If wheel mountings have rusted to a point when they are useless, wheelbarrows can be put into position and supported with a few ornate bricks or a stout piece of wood for the duration of summer.

REUSING OTHER CONTAINERS

- Three car tires wired together in a stack and painted white create an unusual feature. Put summer-flowering plants in a plastic bucket (with holes in its base) and position on bricks placed in the center of the tires.

- In coastal areas, a small old rowboat can become home to plants in containers.

Barrels and casks

Growing strawberries in a large barrel creates an attractive feature on a patio, and one that is sure to capture people's attention. A bonus is that strawberries grown in barrels are not usually at risk from the attentions of snails and slugs. Birds are attracted to them, but netting can be spread over the barrel when the fruits are ripening. In areas where the soil is heavy and continually wet, strawberry plants in barrels have a better chance of survival.

Why grow strawberries in a barrel?

PREPARING A STRAWBERRY BARREL

A strong barrel, with the staves (wooden parts) and metal bands in place and undamaged, is essential for long-term life. Clean the barrel, inside and out, with soapy water, then thoroughly rinse. Here are the steps in preparing your barrel.

Step 2
Between the metal bands drill a series of ½–¾ in (12–18 mm) wide holes. Then, use a keyhole saw to widen them to about 2 in (5 cm). Smooth the edges of the holes.

Step 1
Turn the barrel upside down and drill ¾–1 in (18–25 mm) wide drainage holes in the base. Check that the wood is strong enough to support soil.

Step 5
Fill the tube with coarse pebbles, then add soil to the level of the lowest hole. Systematically, put a strawberry plant into each hole and add more soil. Put a few strawberry plants in the top. Water the soil.

Step 4
Roll 1 in (2.5 cm) mesh wire-netting into a tube 4–5 in (10–13 cm) wide, and long enough to stand on pebbles in the base and rise to just below the barrel's top.

Step 3
Position the barrel upright and place on four stout bricks. Check that the top of the barrel is level; fill the base with 4–6 in (10–15 cm) of large pebbles.

DISPLAYING A CASK ON A TRESTLE

Preparation

- Thoroughly clean the cask, then rinse with water.
- On one side, drill four groups of three holes in the metal bands, forming a 14 in (35 cm) square. Screw the metal bands in place.
- Drill four ½ in (12 mm) holes, 12 in (30 cm) apart and forming an approximate square, in the cask's side. Use a keyhole saw to cut the wood and link them.
- Use a hacksaw to cut the metal bands and open the "window."
- Drill drainage holes on the opposite side.
- Place the cask in the trestle. Fill its base with pebbles, then soil and set plants in place.

Planting options

Casks look good when planted with bushy, as well as trailing, summer-flowering plants. For a display throughout the year, however, drench the planting window with *Sempervivum* plants (Houseleeks). There are many to choose from, including the Hen-and-chicken Houseleek, Common Houseleek and Cobweb Houseleek.

Soil for barrels

Because ornamental barrels are long-term features, use well-drained, loam-based soil to which extra coarse sand has been added. Do not use soft sand. Peat-based soils are not suitable as they tend to compress and, eventually, exclude air and reduce drainage.

Caring for container plants

How easy is it to care for my plants?

Plants grown in containers need regular attention, especially summer-flowering displays in hanging baskets, wall baskets and window boxes, where plants are positioned close together in order to create instant, dense and colorful displays. More permanent plants, such as shrubs and trees, also need care, especially during winter when frost and snow can be a problem. Spring-flowering bulbs planted in tubs are usually trouble-free, however.

FRESH TAP WATER OR FROM A RAINWATER BARREL?

Wherever possible, use fresh water taken directly from an outside water faucet. In winter, of course, the temperature will be low, but as most watering is done during the summer on hanging baskets, window boxes and wall baskets this is not a factor to consider. In earlier years, using water stored in a rainwater barrel was recommended. However, rainwater barrels filled with rainwater channelled off roofs may, in some locations, be contaminated by micro-organisms and impurities.

WATERING PLANTS

Hanging baskets

Plants in hanging baskets soon suffer if watering is neglected. Initially, plants flag and wilt, with flowers being the first to suffer and leaves and stems soon following, the whole plant looking unsightly. If neglect continues, there arrives a time when whatever the amount of water given to plants they will not recover. Therefore, the skill in watering hanging baskets is at all times to keep the soil evenly moist, but never waterlogged.

There are several ways to water hanging baskets (see below). Standing on a stool or stepladder can be dangerous, especially if they are placed on uneven ground and when the basket is high up. Therefore, it is far better to use hose fittings that enable baskets to be watered from ground level.

Fittings for hoses enable water to be gently trickled on soil in hanging baskets. These have plastic tubing with a bent end, so that water is not wasted and can be directed into the basket. Some pieces of equipment have trigger-like mechanisms that enable water to be turned off between each basket, while others just provide a continuous stream of water.

Home-made fittings for hoses are easy to make. All that is needed is a strong, 4 ft (1.2 m) long bamboo cane and a piece of wire from a metal coat hanger. Lay the hose alongside the bamboo cane, with 6–8 in (15–20 cm) protruding at one end. Cut three, 6 in (15 cm) long, pieces of wire to secure the hose to the cane. Use a slightly longer piece to hold the hose's end in a curve.

Where it is difficult to water a hanging basket while suspended, it can be taken down and placed in the top of a plastic bucket and water gently trickled on to the soil. While a hanging basket is in this position it is possible to water the soil several times to ensure it is thoroughly moist. Allow excess moisture to drain before putting the basket back.

If the soil in a hanging basket becomes very dry and when water is applied it immediately runs out, take down the basket and immerse it in water. When bubbles cease to rise from the soil, remove the basket and allow excess water to drain. If plants have become damaged through lack of water, remove wilted flowers.

Window boxes

Window boxes displayed on sills outside sash windows can be watered from inside, and this is ideal for upstairs windows. Window boxes on brackets positioned beneath windows are easier to water from outside. Whenever possible, use specialized extension fittings to hoses so that the job of watering is safe. You should never stand on a box in order to get greater height.

Pots

Where pots are clustered together, the task of watering is made easier by tying the end of a hose to a cane. Slowly dribble water onto the soil; when pots have been newly planted, the soil is easily disturbed by fierce jets of water.

Where shrubs and small trees are planted in clay pots, it is possible to judge if water is required by tapping the pot with a stout wooden dowel. If, when tapped, the pot emits a ringing note, water is needed, whereas if a dull note is produced this indicates that the soil is sufficiently moist already.

FEEDING PLANTS

HANGING BASKETS	WINDOW BOXES, WALL BASKETS AND TROUGHS	TUBS, POTS AND PLANTERS

These are invariably planted with summer-flowering plants and their display is from late spring to early autumn. Foliage plants are often added to the display. Therefore, feeding every two weeks throughout summer is essential.

- The easiest and best way is to add a liquid fertilizer to the water when watering. By this method, roots throughout the basket will be fed. Always water the basket immediately before applying a liquid fertilizer. Never use a fertilizer on dry soil because this may burn and damage the roots of the plants.
- Sometimes, pellets and fertilizer sticks are used, but these tend to cause roots to develop unevenly throughout the container, which may be to the detriment of some plants.

These become homes for many different types of plants throughout the year. During summer, they have the same types of plants as hanging baskets and can be watered and fed in the same way.

- They also create exciting displays in spring, from bulbs and hardy biennials such as double Daisies and Polyanthus. These plants are put in place in autumn and do not need any feeding; bulbs are nature's storehouses of energy.
- Window boxes also have winter displays, which are usually formed of late winter-flowering bulbs, small evergreen shrubs, conifers and trailing plants such as variegated small-leaved *Hedera helix* (Ivies). None of these plants will need feeding, unless they are to be left in a window box for a long time.

Tubs, pots and planters create homes for many different types of plants and this influences their feeding needs.

- Where ephemeral, summer-flowering plants are planted in pots and planters – and especially when in peat-based soil – regular feeding throughout summer is essential to maintain an attractive display.
- Where plants with a more permanent nature are used – and especially when planted in loam-based soil – regular feeding is not so necessary.
- When long-term plants such as shrubs and small trees are used in tubs and large pots, in spring remove about 1 in (2.5 cm) of surface soil – without damaging roots – and replace with fresh potting soil.

DEADHEADING PLANTS

Unsightly dead flower head

Hold the main stem firmly, while bending over and snapping off the stem of a dead flower head. Place it on a compost pile.

Regularly removing dead flowers encourages the development of further blooms. Additionally, if dead flowers are left on plants they encourage the presence of diseases, which might spread throughout all of the plants. Some flowers have a mass of small flowers and these need to be removed individually by either pulling or twisting them sideways. Other flowers, such as Pelargoniums, have clustered flowers attached to a single stalk. Either snap the stem sideways or use scissors or a sharp knife.

ENCOURAGING BUSHINESS

Some plants have a natural, bushy habit and do not have to be encouraged to develop masses of stems. They have stems which arise from leaf-joints without anything being done to the plant. Other plants need to have their terminal shoots, or growing tips, removed.

Fuchsias, when young, benefit from having shoots nipped off to just above a leaf-joint. This encourages the development of further shoots; it may need to be done several times. It is essential to nip shoots back to just above a leaf-joint; if long, bare, pieces of stem are left, they will decay and die back.

Pinch out the tip between finger and thumb

Nipping off a growing tip encourages the growth of side shoots lower down.

COPING WITH LATE FROSTS

Late spring frosts soon damage young, tender shoots on summer-flowering plants. Some plants, such as those grown in hanging baskets, are especially at risk and if a frost is forecast a few sheets of newspaper pushed over the plants and between the supporting chains will be helpful. However, if a severe frost is forecast, put the entire basket in a frost-proof greenhouse or shed. Summer-flowering plants in window boxes are also at risk and these can also be protected by a few sheets of newspaper. Protecting tender evergreen shrubs from severe frost is described on page 74, as well as preventing the soil becoming saturated with water, freezing and damaging the roots.

Protect plants from the danger of late frosts by placing a few sheets of newspaper over them.

Plants in window boxes also need protection from frost by covering with newspaper.

Winter protection

Many slightly tender shrubs and trees can be grown in temperate climates if given protection from frost and sudden dips in temperature during winter. Deciduous shrubs and trees shed their leaves in autumn and overwinter as bare stems and branches, but evergreen types are more at risk and these are the ones that especially need protection. Small ones can be moved into a frost-proof greenhouse or conservatory. Covering them in straw is an alternative.

PROTECTING TENDER EVERGREENS

Whether tender shrubs or trees are growing in tubs, large pots or Versailles planters, they all can be protected by covering the foliage in straw. As soon as the temperature falls and frost is forecast, cover and protect all your tender shrubs and trees. Clearly, the need to protect a plant depends on the local climate. Exposure to coastal areas – some engulfed in warm water, others known for their cold temperatures – can also have an influence. Throughout the winter, regularly check the straw and remove it as soon as the weather starts to improve. If it is left in position too long, there may be a risk of the plant being damaged when growth resumes.

1 *Insert about five 5 ft (1.5 m) long pliable canes about 5 in (13 cm) deep in compost close to the tub's edge. Gently pull the tops of the canes together to form a teepee, so that they cross 6–8 in (15–20 cm) from the top. Use strong string to hold them together and, if possible, flex and bend the canes outwards so that all the plant's foliage is within their area. If a few young shoots extend outwards it is not usually a problem, as later they can be covered in a layer of straw.*

2 *Starting from the top of the teepee of canes, spread a thick layer of straw evenly over the entire surface. It is usually necessary to push straw between a few canes, so that it is temporarily held in place. As an alternative to straw, you can use hay, but this is not as weather-resistant as straw. Secure the end of a ball of string to the top and start winding downwards, in a slight spiral. Add further straw as the spiral proceeds. Continue adding straw until the bottom is reached, when the end of the string can be tied to a cane.*

Problems with snow

A flurry and light coating of snow on leaves of evergreen shrubs is usually not a problem; it can be easily dusted off with a soft brush or a branch tapped with a cane to remove it. Essentially, it must be removed before it freezes and subsequent falls of snow build up on it, causing branches to become weighed down and, eventually, misshapen.

Bamboos chosen for growing in containers are usually sufficiently hardy to withstand cold weather in temperate climates, but heavy snowfalls bend the canes over and, if not removed, cause them to become misshapen.

PROTECTING SOIL

Soil in tubs and large pots is at risk of becoming too wet during the winter months. Plants are not active and excessive water damages the soil and the plant's roots, especially when frozen. Therefore, in late autumn place two bricks on the soil (above) to ensure that water drains away. Cover the soil with plastic sheeting (right). Remove it in late winter.

PROTECTING CONTAINERS

Some containers – such as those formed of thin plastic or fiberglass – give little protection to soil in containers during winter and consequently soil balls and roots are at risk. Thin metal containers, although having a trendy and modern appearance, also put roots at risk. Covering these containers in sacking that encapsulates straw gives protection, but, if soaked in rain which then freezes, acts like a refrigerator, so keep a careful eye on weather conditions and be ready to take the container under cover temporarily (see below).

Storing pots and tubs in winter

Winter plays havoc with containers and, wherever possible, you should store them under cover. If this is not possible, however, it is a good idea to cover them with plastic to prevent water penetrating them. It is a combination of water and freezing temperatures that cause most trouble, although water at any time of year puts wood at risk.

Attaching brackets and hooks

General deterioration, strong wind and weak and crumbling brickwork makes brackets that support hanging baskets, window boxes and other wall-mounted containers at risk of failing and causing damage to plants and people. Yearly, in autumn or spring and before putting containers in place, check that hardware is secure and that brackets are strong enough for another season. Never take risks as displays could be ruined and someone severely injured.

How strong should the fixings be?

GETTING THE HARDWARE RIGHT

Using secure hardware in walls is absolutely essential; two of the best types to use are illustrated below:

For attaching to plasterboard walls, perhaps in a porch or vestibule

For attaching to brick walls, outdoors and indoors

POSITIONING HANGING BASKETS

Practical positions

✔ Against walls and on wide patios and terraces.

✔ Where passers-by cannot knock them with their heads or shoulders.

✔ Where they will not be buffeted by strong winds that damage plants and loosen supporting brackets.

Impractical positions

✘ Alongside narrow paths and where water can drip onto plants and people passing beneath.

✘ Where plants are difficult to reach for watering and routine care.

✘ Where the basket over-hangs a sidewalk.

SECURING HANGING BASKETS

Securing cup-hooks to bargeboards or fascias: this is only practical on bungalows, where the eaves extend 15 in (38 cm) beyond the brickwork of the house walls. Additionally, it is only possible where the bargeboard or fascia is made of strong wood, rather than of plastic or plasterboard. Always use strong eye-hooks for this purpose.

Securing brackets to wooden walls: some homes are constructed of a wooden framework, with the addition of wooden or plastic cladding. When securing a bracket, check that the desired position is structurally sound and able to give support. Mark the position, and use a thin drill to create a pilot hole to provide the screw with guidance and to prevent the wood being split by the width of the screw. Nevertheless, the bracket must be quite secure.

Supporting chains: where possible – and especially for large, outdoor hanging baskets – use hanging baskets that are suspended from four chains rather than three. Then, each spring, check that the chains are strong and not corroded and weakened. Also remember to inspect the hooks that secure them to the basket and hook at the top.

ATTACHING WINDOW BOX BRACKETS

When attaching window box brackets to a wall they must be strong, secure, attractive, level and positioned centrally under a window. On casement windows, their distance beneath a sill is important to enable the window to open freely over plants.

1 *First, measure down from the sill and mark on the wall the top of the first bracket – the depth of the window box plus 5–8 in (15–20 cm). Position the brackets so that the box will be supported about one-third in from each side, yet in the middle of the window.*

2 *Mark the drilling positions on the wall and, using a masonry drill, make the holes. Push one of the wall anchors into each hole and then use galvanized screws to hold the bracket firmly in the correct place.*

3 *Hold the other bracket in place (an equal distance in from the other side of the window) and, using a carpenter's level, mark the drilling holes. Insert wall anchors and screw the bracket in place. Check that the window box will not be able to fall forward and off the brackets (most brackets have lipped edges).*

CRIME-BUSTING

There are security devices available that prevent hanging baskets and their displays being stolen. Alternatively, twist some strong wire around the supporting hook.

SAFETY WITH ELECTRIC DRILLS

When using a corded-electric drill, always check that there is a circuit-breaker installed that will instantly cut off the power should a electrical short be created.

Pests and diseases

How do I keep my container plants healthy?

Hanging baskets, window boxes and wall baskets, as well as pots and tubs, become packed with tender plants during summer, creating succulent feasts for pests. They are also excellent places for diseases. Some pests, such as snails, slugs, woodlice and earwigs, have a crawling nature, while others fly and soon spread damage from one container to another. Vigilance is essential, and when watering and looking after plants check that pests and diseases are not present – and take control measures immediately.

Cyclamen mites

Often seen on Cyclamen and Pelargoniums indoors, and therefore occasionally in hanging baskets in vestibules. **Pick off infected leaves or destroy severely infested plants.**

Red spider mites

These sometimes infest plants in vestibules. They suck sap, causing bleached areas. **Increase ventilation, mist-spray leaves and spray with a systemic insecticide.**

Gray mold

Often known as botrytis, this creates fluffy, mold-like growths on flowers and soft stems. **Cut off and destroy infected plants. Increase ventilation and use a fungicide.**

Viruses

These infect many plants, causing discoloration and distortion. Leaves may have white streaks. **There is no cure: throw away and burn badly infected plants and spray with insecticides to kill sucking pests such as aphids that spread them.**

Caterpillars

They chew soft leaves and stems, making them unsightly. **Pick off caterpillars as soon as they are seen – and destroy. Additionally, spray plants with an insecticide at ten-day intervals. At the end of summer, pull up and burn all rubbish to prevent infestations during the following year.**

Powdery mildew

This sometimes coats leaves with a white, powdery deposit. It is occasionally seen on plants indoors, so check plants in vestibules. **Pick off infected leaves, improve ventilation and spray with a fungicide.**

Woodlice

They climb walls and infest wall baskets and window boxes, as well as plants in pots, tubs and grow bags on a patio. They mainly come out of hiding at night and chew leaves, stems, flowers and roots. **Dust with an insecticide.**

Whitefly

These are small, white, moth-like insects that flutter from one plant to another, sucking sap and causing mottling. **Spray with an insecticide. Control is difficult.**

SAFETY FIRST

Chemicals sprayed on plants in gardens and vestibules are lethal to pests and therefore must be treated with a great deal of respect.

- Carefully follow the manufacturer's instructions. Don't be tempted to use chemicals at a higher than recommended concentration as they will not be more effective – and may even damage plants.

- Don't mix two different chemicals, unless recommended.

- Before using, check that the chemical will not damage specific plants.

- Keep all chemicals away from children and pets. Don't transfer chemicals into bottles that children might believe to contain a refreshing drink.

- Don't use the same equipment for both weedkillers and insecticides.

- Thoroughly wash all spraying equipment after use.

Thrips

These infest plants in vestibules and porches, where they hop and flit from one plant to another. They cause streaking and mottling. **Use an insecticide.**

Aphids

These are pernicious pests that suck sap, causing mottling and distortion. Blackfly sometimes infest plants, especially nasturtiums. **Spray plants with an insecticide every 10–14 days throughout summer.**

Earwigs

These are pernicious pests, hiding during the day and chewing and tearing leaves, flowers and soft stems at night. They attack plants in window boxes and wall baskets, as well as in hanging baskets if they can be reached. **Pick off and destroy them; also spray with an insecticide.**

Snails

They have similar appetites to slugs, and infest plants in the same way. **Pick them off and use baits and traps.**

Slugs

These are nature's stealth pests; they hide during the day and come out at night to decimate plants in tubs, pots, grow bags and other containers on patios. They also climb walls to get at plants in window boxes and wall baskets. **Pick them off and destroy them. It is also possible to use baits and traps, such as saucers filled with beer and sugar. Take care, however, that domestic pets, as well as wild animals, cannot reach the baits or traps.**

Glossary

Annual
A plant that is raised from seed and completes its life cycle within one growing season. Some annuals are half-hardy in temperate zones and therefore raised in gentle warmth in late winter or early spring. They are planted into containers in late spring or early summer, when all risk of frost has passed.

Barrels
Wooden containers used during earlier years to transport all manner of materials, including beer, flour, tobacco and gunpowder. They range from a pin (4½ gallons/20 litres) to a butt (108 gallons/490 litres). Today, barrels are either cut in half to form tubs, or left intact and drilled so that plants such as strawberries can be grown in them.

Biennial
A plant that takes two growing seasons to grow from seed and to produce flowers. Many spring-flowering plants grown in containers are biennial, such as Wallflowers and Daisies.

Bulb
Formed of overlapping, fleshy, modified leaves, creating a food-storage organ that, when given the right conditions, develops leaves and flowers. Many spring-flowering plants in containers are bulbs, including Hyacinths and Daffodils.

Courtyards
Originally, open areas surrounded by buildings or walls, perhaps inside a castle. Nowadays, they are paved areas at the rear of a building and surrounded by a wall.

Crocks
Pieces of broken clay pots used to cover drainage holes in containers. They are placed concave side downwards.

Deadheading
The removal of faded flowers to encourage the development of further blooms.

Drip-tray
Integral with plastic-type hanging baskets to prevent water dripping on floors and plants beneath.

Grow bag
Originally introduced to grow tomatoes on disease-infected soil, but now widely used as homes for many flowering plants, as well as herbs and vegetables.

Herbaceous perennials
Plants that die down to soil level in autumn and send up fresh shoots in spring. Some of these can be grown in tubs and other large containers on a patio.

Jardinière
A large, decorative stand or pot that is used to display plants.

Loam-based soil
Formed mainly of fertile topsoil, with the addition of coarse sand, peat and fertilizers.

Patio
The Spanish used this term to describe an inner court, open to the sky and surrounded by a building. The term was introduced by the Spanish to North America, where it became to mean any paved area around a dwelling.

Peat-based soil
Formed mainly of peat, with the addition of fertilizers.

Perlite
A moisture-retentive material added to soil.

Reconstituted stone
Used to construct a wide range of plant containers and ornaments. It mellows to a pleasing color.

Sink gardens
An unusual way to grow small plants such as miniature conifers, alpine plants and bulbs. Stone sinks are best, but modified glazed types can also be used.

Sphagnum moss
A type of moss, earlier and widely used to line wire-framed hanging baskets to assist in moisture retention and to prevent soil spilling out of the container.

Terraces
Open, paved areas immediately outside a house. Sometimes, they are on several levels and united by flights of stems. Usually they have a firm, hard surface, but earlier long and large ones were grassed.

Terracotta
A hardy, brownish-red material formed of clay, fine sand and, occasionally, pulverized pottery waste. This is made into containers – usually unglazed – for plants.

Urn
A vase of varying shape and ornamentation made of fiberglass, metal, plastic or reconstituted stone. Because of the limited amount of soil they can hold, they are mainly used for summer-flowering plants.

Veranda
A term derived from India, describing a gallery at ground level and on one side of a house (occasionally completely surrounding it). The roof is sloped to shed water and the sides are partly or wholly open on the garden side.

Versailles planter
A large, square-sided container originated at Versailles, France. Early ones were made of lead or slate, while modern types are usually made of fiberglass or wood.

Vermiculite
A moisture-retentive material added to soil.

Index

Acknowledgments

AG&G Books would like to thank the following suppliers for their contribution: **B&Q plc**, Head Office, Portswood House, 1 Hampshir Corporate Park, Chandlers Ford, Eastleigh, Hampshire SO53 3YX, UK, Tel: 01703 256256, **Barbary Pots**, www.barbarypots.co.uk, **Forest Garden plc (Builder Center)**, www.forestgarden.co.uk, **Thompson & Morgan**, Quality Seedsmen Since 1855, *brings the finest quality flower and vegetable seed and flower plant varieties to the home gardener*, Thompson & Morgan (UK) Ltd, Poplar Lane, Ipswich, Suffolk, IP8 3BU, **Windowbox.com**, www.windowbox.com. Photographs: AG&G Books (cover and pages 2, 3, 12, 43CL, 47BL, 50, 52TL AND WINDOW BOXES: PAINTED PINE, DECORATED WOOD, TERRACOTTA AND PLASTIC LEAD EFFECT, 54, 56, 58, 60, 61, 62 EXCEPT TL, 63, 64 POT ETC OPTIONS: ALL PICTURES EXCEPT THOSE LISTED HERE, 65, 69 and 70), B&Q (page 64 POT ETC OPTIONS: LARGE PLASTIC POT, TERRACOTTA 'LONG TOMS', FLARED-SHAPE TERRACOTTA POT, DECORATED GLAZED POT AND GLAZED CERAMIC POTS), Barbary Pots (page 64 POT ETC OPTIONS: LARGE HANDMADE TERRACOTTA URN AT CENTER), Peter Chan (page 37BL,BC AND BR), John Douch (page 37CR), Forest Garden (pages 52 WINDOW BOXES: PINE LOG EFFECT AND LATTICE FRONT and 62TL), Garden Matters (pages 17CR AND BL, 34BL, 35CL and 44CR), Garden World Images (page 31TC AND TR), Peter McHoy (pages 16C, 18BR, 20TL, 22CR, 24C, 25BC, 26TL AND CR, 27CL, 28TL, TC AND CR, 29CR, BL AND BC, 32BL, 33TR AND C, 34CL, C AND CR, 35TL, TC, TR AND BL, 36CR, BL AND BC, 38BL, 39TL, TC, CL AND BL, 40C AND BR, 41TL, 42C, CR AND BR, 43BC, 44C, BC AND BR, 45TC, TR AND BC, 47C, 48BR and 49C AND BC), David Squire (all pictures except those listed here), Thompson & Morgan (pages 16CR, BL, BC AND BR, 17TL, TC, TR, BR, AND BC, 18TL, TC, TR, C, CR AND BL, 19 EXCEPT BC, 20TC, BC, BR, 21 EXCEPT CR, 22CL, 46, 47TC, CL AND BC) and Windowbox.com (page 52 WINDOW BOXES: CEDAR, METAL FRAME, WHITE-PAINTED STEEL, RECONSTITUTED STONE, PLASTIC KIT A WOVEN WILLOW).